OUTLOOK FOR OUTDOOR RECREATION

in the Northern United States

A Technical Document Supporting the
Northern Forest Futures Project
with Projections through 2060

ABSTRACT

We develop projections of participation and use for 17 nature-based outdoor recreation activities through 2060 for the Northern United States. Similar to the 2010 Resources Planning Act (RPA) assessment, this report develops recreation projections under futures wherein population growth, socioeconomic conditions, land use changes, and climate are allowed to change over time.

Findings indicate that outdoor recreation will likely remain a key part of the region's future social and economic fabric. The number of participants in 14 of the 17 recreation activities is projected to increase over the next five decades. In about two-thirds of 17 activities, the participation rate will likely decrease, but population growth would ensure increases in the number of adult participants. Some climate futures could lead to participant decreases for certain activities. Hunting, snowmobiling, and undeveloped skiing appear to be the only activities for which a decrease in participants is likely. Total days of participation would generally follow the pattern of participant numbers. With the exceptions of hunting, visiting primitive areas, and whitewater activities, snowmobiling, undeveloped skiing, total days are expected to increase for the remaining 14 activities, some less so than others because of climate differences.

Keywords: outdoor recreation, participation rate, climate change, double-hurdle model, recreation projections

---

How to cite this publication: Bowker, J.M.; Askew, Ashley E. 2013. Outlook for Outdoor Recreation in the Northern United States. A Technical Document Supporting the Northern Forest Futures Project with Projections through 2060. Gen. Tech. Rep. NRS-120. Newtown Square, PA: U.S. Department of Agriculture, Forest Service, Northern Research Station. 62 p.

Manuscript received for publication: September 2012

Published by: For additional copies:
USDA Forest Service   U.S. Forest Service
Northern Research Station   Publications Distribution
11 Campus Blvd, Suite 200   359 Main Road
Newtown Square, PA 19073   Delaware, OH 43015

September 2013   Fax: 740-368-0152

Visit our homepage at: http://www.nrs.fs.fed.us

Outlook for Outdoor Recreation in the Northern United States

A Technical Document Supporting the Northern Forest Futures Project

with Projections through 2060

J. M. Bowker and Ashley E. Askew

J. M. BOWKER, RESEARCH SOCIAL SCIENTIST
U.S. Forest Service, Southern Research Station
320 Green Street
Athens, GA 30602
mbowker@fs.fed.us
706-559-4271

ASHLEY E. ASKEW, DOCTORAL CANDIDATE
University of Georgia, Department of Statistics
101 Cedar Street
Athens, GA 30602

C O N T E N T S

Outlook for Outdoor Recreation in the Northern United States

INTRODUCTION

This report addresses a major question considered relevant to the Northern Forests Futures Project, namely, "How will population growth, along with changing socioeconomic conditions, demographics, land uses, and climate, influence associated demand for natural resource-based recreation?" The question is addressed through an analysis of natural resource-based outdoor recreation demand for the 20 states that make up the U.S. North (Fig. 1), a region that is bounded by Maine, Maryland, Missouri, and Minnesota.

The report mirrors and extends previous studies that were part of the recent U.S. Forest Service 2010 Resources Planning Act (RPA) assessment (Bowker et al. 2012) and the Southern Forest Futures Project (Bowker et al., in press). Specifically, we developed regional projections of participation and use for 17 natural resource-based outdoor-recreation activities, or activity composites (Table 1), through 2060. The report was also designed to complement a concurrent study of current and recent trends in outdoor recreation in the North (Cordell et al. 2012).

Intermountain

Great Plains

North Central

Pacific Northwest

Northeast

PACIFIC COAST

Pacific Southwest

ROCKY MOUNTAIN

NORTH

SOUTH

Southeast

South Central

FIGURE 1

Regions for the 2010 U.S. Resources
Planning Act (RPA) assessment.

PARTICIPATION AND USE

We defined a participant in an outdoor recreation activity as an adult resident over the age of 16 who engaged in that activity at least once in the previous 12 months. Participation is a general indicator of the size of a given recreation market, and it also can be a gauge of public interest. Land managers and legislators can benefit from knowing how many people participate in a given recreation activity as well as how participation could change over time and affect both public support and potential ecological and social carrying capacities (Dale and Weaver 1974, Manning 1997). For example, if more than 80 percent of the population participates in hiking but just 4 percent participate in snowmobiling, public resource management agencies and private land managers may see a greater need for hiking trails than for snowmobiling trails. Measures of participation, either per capita (participation rates) or in absolute numbers of participants, provide the broadest measure of a recreation market.

Table 1—Outdoor recreation activities for 2008 by participants, participation rate, days, and days per participant for Northern residents

Activity	Participants (millions)[b]	Percent Participating	Days (millions)[c]	Days per Participant
Developed Site Use				
Visiting Developed Sites – family gatherings, picnicking, developed camping	80.5	82.5	943	11.7
Visiting Interpretive Sites – nature centers, zoos, historic sites, prehistoric sites	67.0	68.6	516	7.7
Observing Nature				
Birding – viewing and/or photographing birds	37.2	38.2	3,696	99.8
Viewing[d] – viewing, photography, study, or nature gathering related to fauna, flora, or natural settings	79.5	81.5	13,925	175.7
Backcountry Activities				
Challenge Activities – caving, mountain biking, mountain climbing, rock climbing	9.4	9.5	37.7	3.9
Equestrian	5.8	5.9	72.3	12.6
Hiking – day hiking	32.4	32.7	723.8	22.4
Visiting Primitive Areas – backpacking, primitive camping, wilderness	36.1	36.7	415	11.4
Motorized Activities				
Motorized off-road use	17.3	17.6	282.8	16.4
Motorized snow use (snowmobiling)	7.0	7.1	54.8	7.9
Motorized water use	26.1	26.8	378.8	14.7
Hunting and fishing				
Hunting – small game, big game, migratory bird, other	11.3	11.7	209.6	18.8
Fishing – anadramous, coldwater, saltwater, warmwater	28.7	29.6	515.7	18.1
Non-Motorized Winter Activities				
Downhill Skiing – downhill skiing, snowboarding	11.6	11.6	81.3	7.0
Undeveloped Skiing – cross-country skiing, snowshoeing	4.8	4.8	32.1	6.7
Non-Motorized Water Activities				
Swimming – swimming, snorkeling, surfing, diving, visiting beaches or watersides	61.7	63.3	1,376	22.2
Floating – canoeing, kayaking, rafting, sailing	18.2	18.7	124	6.8

Source: NSRE 2005-2009. Versions 1 to 4 (January 2005 to April 2009). n=24,073.

[a]Activities are individual or activity composites derived from the NSRE.

[b]Participants are determined by the product of the average weighted frequency of participation by activity for NSRE data from 2005-2009 and the adult (>16) population in the US during 2008 (235.4 million).

[c]Days are determined by the product of the weighted conditional average days per adult participant and the number of participants by activity for NSRE data from 2005-2009.

[d]Including birding.

A second measure of recreation use is consumption or participation intensity. Consumption can be measured in number of times, days, visits, or trips within a time span, such as a 12-month period. The U.S. Forest Service has used such consumption measures as recreation visitor days and national forest visits. Consumption measures of participation (knowing how often and for how long people engage in an activity) provide an important additional dimension for resource managers who need to know how best to allocate resources, such as campsites, and whether to plan new ones.

Participation and consumption at the regional level provide the broadest measures of an outdoor recreation market. The consumption measure used in this study is the number of days in the previous year that an adult resident of the Northern United States reported engaging in a specific activity. A *day*, in this study, follows the National Survey on Recreation and the Environment (NSRE) definition of an activity day—any amount of time spent on an activity on a given day, whether or not that activity was the primary reason for the outdoors visit. Hence, camping at an improved facility for one night would constitute two days of camping. A person may engage in more than one activity per day, and thus, a person's activity day total per year may not exceed 365 for any specific activity but it may do so when all activities are combined (Cordell 2012).

These two metrics—participation and consumption—are origin based, meaning that they result from household-level surveying. There is no additional information on exactly where the respondent engaged in the participation for any activity, although research shows that the vast majority of outdoor recreation takes place within a few hours' drive of home (Hall and Page 1999). Participation rates and participant numbers for 2008, along with total days spent participating and average days per participant, for the 17 outdoor recreation activities examined in this study are displayed in Table 1.

A history of outdoor recreation trends is an important indicator of what may happen in the near future (Cordell 2012, Hall et al. 2009). However, simple descriptive statistics or trends do not formally address underlying factors and associations that may be driving these trends. Thus, a trend may be of limited value as an indicator if the time horizon is long or if the driving factors are expected to deviate substantially from historical levels. Trend analysis, therefore, can be supplemented with projection models that relate participation directly to factors known to influence participation behavior. The projection models then can be used in conjunction with external projections of relevant factors, including population growth, to simulate future recreation participation and consumption.

Such modeling allows changes in recreation participation and consumption behavior to be assessed in light of large changes in demographics, economic conditions, land use, climate, and other previously unseen influential factors.

Previous research has demonstrated that race, ethnicity, gender, age, income, supply, and proximity to settings may be related to the rate of outdoor recreation participation as well as the participation intensity or consumption (Bowker et al. 1999, Bowker et al. 2006, Cicchetti 1973, Hof and Kaiser 1983b, Leeworthy et al. 2005). Along with distance and quality descriptors and other factors, these have been used to explain visits to specific sites (Bowker et al. 2007, Bowker et al. 2010, Englin and Shonkwiler 1995, Ovaskainen et al. 2001). Reliable information about these factors is often available from external sources such as the U.S. Census Bureau or from parallel research efforts to model and simulate influential variables into the future. Such information thus can be available long before recreation survey results are published.

A two-step approach was used to project participation and consumption of 17 traditional outdoor recreation activities (Table 1). The first step, model estimation, focused on developing regional level statistical models of adult per capita participation and days of participation (conditional on being a participant) for each activity, with the participation model describing the probability of an individual participating in a specified activity and the consumption model describing the number of days of participation for those activities in which an individual participated. This information improves understanding of the influences on individual recreation choices or behaviors and of the way that individual recreation choices or behavior might respond to changes in underlying factors such as demographics, resource availability, and climate.

The second step, or simulation step, combined the estimated models with external projections of relevant explanatory variables to generate estimated per capita participation probabilities and conditional expected days of participation for each activity at 10-year intervals to 2060. These were combined with population projections to develop regional estimates for each activity, which were used to create indices by which 2008 baseline estimates of participants and days of participation for the various activities (Table 1) could be scaled.

The resulting indices of estimated adult participants for each of the 17 activities and days of annual participation are presented for an updated version of an emissions storyline (high economic growth with moderate population growth) from the Intergovernmental Panel on Climate Change in combination with three associated climate futures that were derived from the three general circulation models—CGCM3.1 and CSIROMK3.5 downloaded from the World Climate Research Program Climate Model Intercomparison Project 3 website, and MIROC3.2 downloaded from the IPCC Data Distribution Centre (Joyce et al., in press)—described below.

MODEL DEVELOPMENT

The conditions during the projection period for this report are based on one of three scenarios used for the 2010 RPA assessment (U.S. Department of Agriculture Forest Service 2012). Three RPA scenarios were developed to describe alternative national and county-level futures which were linked to emissions storylines developed during the Intergovernmental Panel on Climate Change third and fourth assessments (IPCC 2007), thereby providing context and quantitative linkages between national and global trends including assumptions and projections of global population growth, economic growth, bioenergy use, and climate (Alcamo et al. 2003, IPCC 2007, Nakićenović et al. 2000).

Table 2—Key characteristics of the Resources Planning Act (RPA) scenarios.

Characteristic[a]	Scenario RPA A1B	Scenario RPA A2	Scenario RPA B2
General global description	Globalization, economic convergence	Regionalism, less trade	Slow change, localized solutions
Global real GDP[b] growth (2010-2060)	High (6.2X)[c]	Low (3.2X)	Medium (3.5X)
Global population growth (2010-2060)	Medium (1.3X)	High (1.7X)	Medium (1.4X)
IPCC global expansion of primary biomass energy production	High	Medium	Medium
U.S. GDP growth (2006-2060)	High (3.3X)	Medium (2.6X)	Low (2.2X)
U.S. population growth (2006-2060)	Medium (1.5X)	High (1.7X)	Low (1.3X)

[a] Global characteristics are based on Intergovernmental Panel on Climate Change (2007) emissions assumptions. U.S. characteristics are from the 2010 Resources Planning Act (RPA) assessment.

[b] GDP = Gross Domestic Product.

[c] Numbers in parentheses are the factors of change in the projection period. For example, world GDP (gross domestic product) increases by a factor of 6.2 times between 2010 and 2060 for scenario RPA A1B.

Of the three storylines—A1B (high economic growth, moderate population growth), A2 (moderate economic growth, high population growth), and B2 (low economic growth, low population growth)—only A1B was used for this study. Table 2 summarizes key global and national characteristics of all three storylines.

Population projections were developed for each RPA scenario. Projections for the original A1B storyline were based on the 1990 Census.

These were updated to align with the 2004 Census population series for 2000 to 2050 (U.S. Census Bureau 2004), with an extrapolation to 2060. The population projections for the original A2 and B2 were updated to begin at the same starting point, in year 2000, and to then follow a projection path that maintains the same proportional relationship to A1B as in the original projections. Figure 2 illustrates the population projections for the three updated storylines relative to historical population trends (Zarnoch et al. 2010).

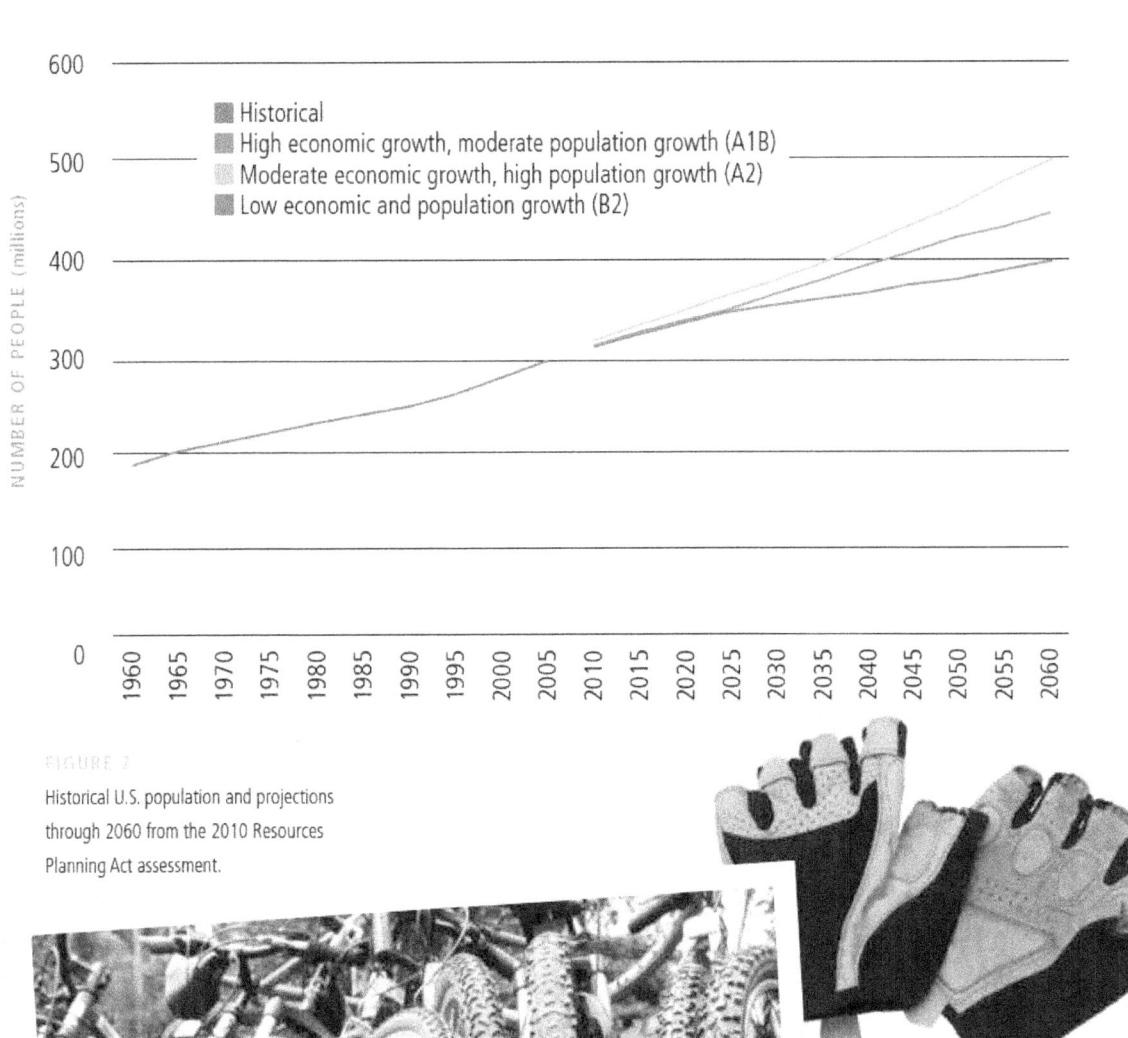

Legend:
- Historical
- High economic growth, moderate population growth (A1B)
- Moderate economic growth, high population growth (A2)
- Low economic and population growth (B2)

Y-axis: NUMBER OF PEOPLE (millions) — 0, 100, 200, 300, 400, 500, 600

X-axis: 1960, 1965, 1970, 1975, 1980, 1985, 1990, 1995, 2000, 2005, 2010, 2015, 2020, 2025, 2030, 2035, 2040, 2045, 2050, 2055, 2060

FIGURE 2
Historical U.S. population and projections through 2060 from the 2010 Resources Planning Act assessment.

Macroeconomic trends—such as Gross Domestic Product (GDP), disposable personal income, and labor productivity—critically influence the supply and demand of renewable resources, and thus, also influence recreation demand. Because the original storylines were based on economic data from the early 1990s, GDP projections were updated to start with the official GDP value for 2006 (U.S. Department of Commerce 2008a). GDP growth rates, provided by a commissioned report, were applied to develop an adjusted projection for A1B. Revised A2 and B2 projections maintained the same proportional relationship among the three storylines as defined by the original GDP projections (U.S. Department of Agriculture Forest Service 2012). Figure 3 shows the differences among the three projections for updated GDP in comparison to historical records.

Projections of personal income and disposable personal income also were developed. U.S. 2006 personal income and disposable personal income data were used to start the updated projection for A1B (U.S. Department of Commerce 2008b). A2 and B2 projections for personal income and disposable personal income maintained the same proportional relationship that was used to calculate the trajectories for GDP. The national disposable personal income and personal income projections were then disaggregated to the county level (U.S. Department of Agriculture Forest Service 2012).

FIGURE 3

Historical U.S. gross domestic product (GDP) and projections through 2060 from the 2010 Resources Planning Act assessment (2006 U.S. dollars).

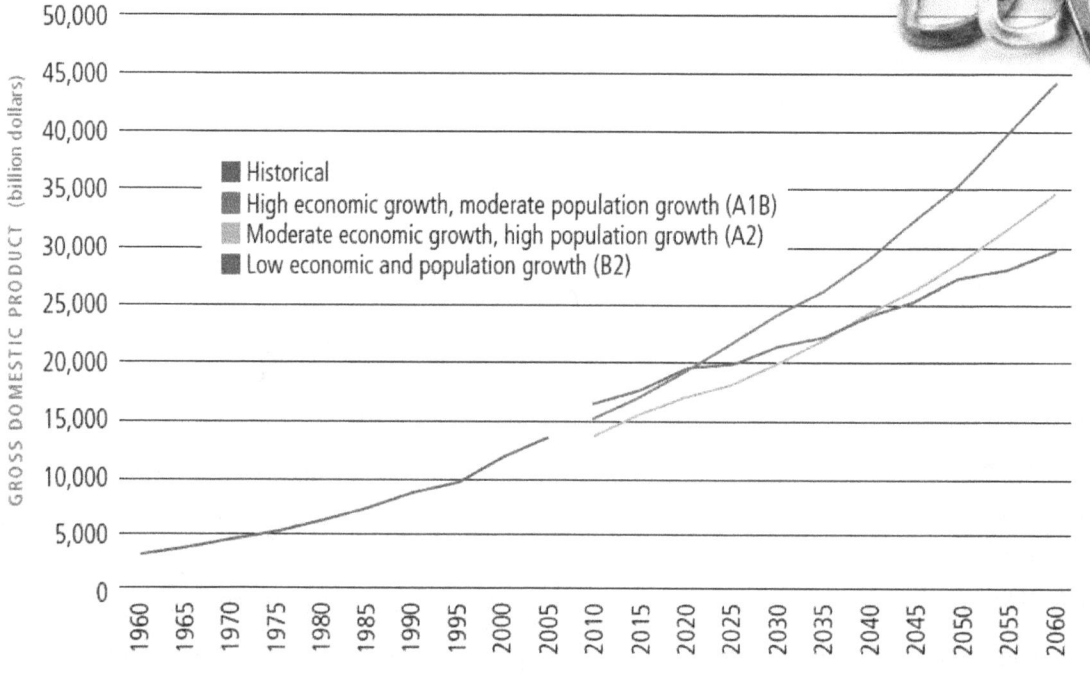

The RPA projections were completed before the global economic downturn that began in 2008. Because data from 2006 were the most recent, that year was chosen as the base year for economic variables. The projection trend line from 2006 to 2010 does not account for the downturn in GDP and other economic variables through 2010, creating a discontinuity in the early years of the projection period. Long-term projections are not intended to predict economic ups and downs, meaning that periodic economic recessions would not be a part of the projected 50-year trend. Although the recent global recession was severe, the range of alternatives included in the RPA assessment have varying rates of economic growth, both for the United States and globally, providing a robust set of projections across the range of potential futures.

Land use change is a key factor in outdoor recreation participation and demand. Land use change was projected for all counties in the contiguous United States in five major land use classes: pasture, cropland, forest land, rangeland, and urban and developed uses (Wear 2011). Within these categories, no land use change was assumed to occur on Federal land; additionally, uses were held constant over the projection period for water area, enrolled Conservation Reserve Program lands, and utility corridors for fuels, water, and electricity.

The projected changes in major land uses at the national level for A1B are summarized in Figure 4. This pattern of change is similar for A2 and B2, but with smaller changes than A1B (U.S. Department of Agriculture Forest Service 2012).

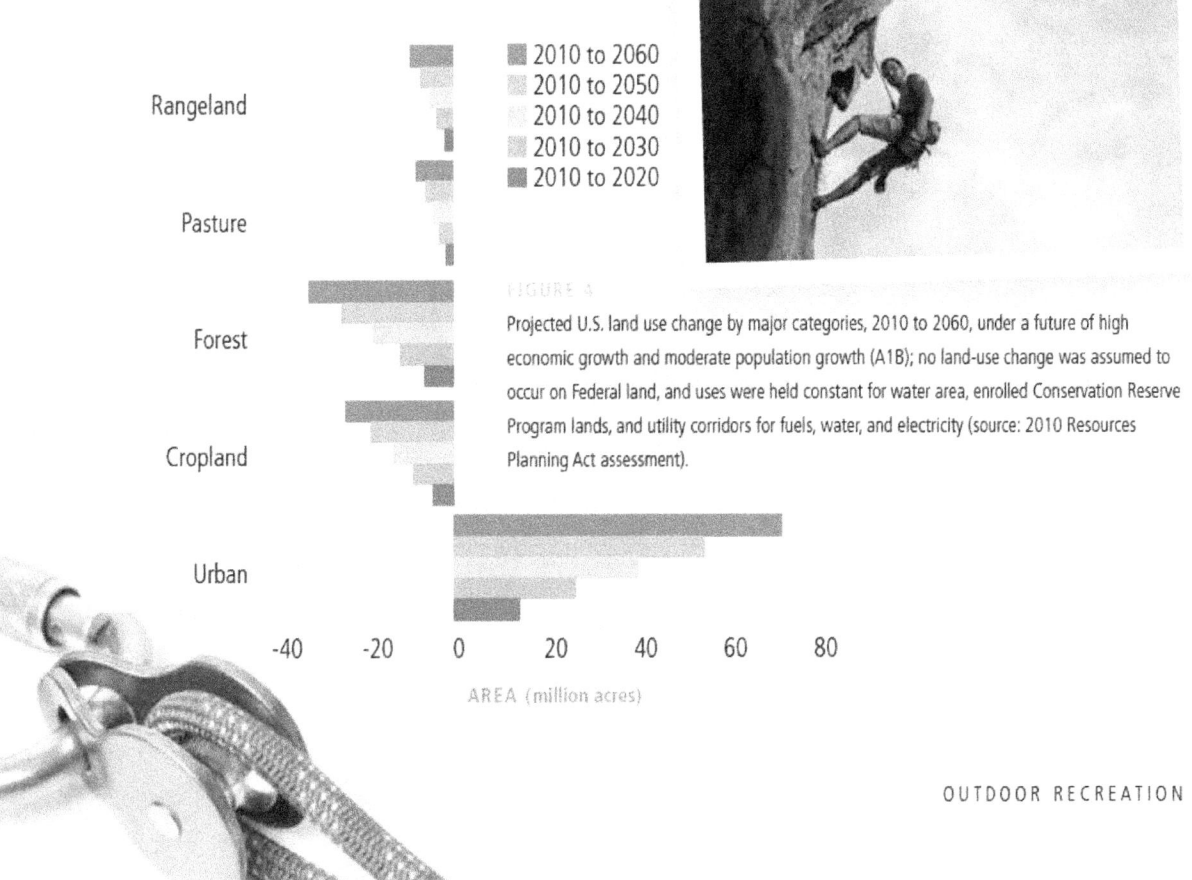

FIGURE 4

Projected U.S. land use change by major categories, 2010 to 2060, under a future of high economic growth and moderate population growth (A1B); no land-use change was assumed to occur on Federal land, and uses were held constant for water area, enrolled Conservation Reserve Program lands, and utility corridors for fuels, water, and electricity (source: 2010 Resources Planning Act assessment).

In all, increases in urban and developed uses are expected to be the dominant force in land use change, with other land uses projected to lose area accordingly. The highest rate of urbanization is associated with A1B and the lowest with B2, suggesting that strong growth in personal income combined with moderate population growth creates more development pressure than population growth alone. Urban and developed area would increase by 69 million acres from 2010 to 2060 for A1B, almost doubling the amount of urban area over the projection period (Wear 2011).

Forest land would decrease by almost 31 million acres over the projection period under A1B, compared to 16 million acres under B2 (Wear 2011). The South (Fig. 5) is projected to experience the largest decrease in forest area by 2060, about 17 million acres in A1B.

These large losses reflect both a history of comparatively abundant forest resources and a future likelihood of comparatively high population growth and urbanization. The North has the second largest loss of forest land in A1B (almost 10 million acres), followed by smaller losses in the Rocky Mountains and Pacific Coast. Although losses of forest land are smaller in A2 and B2, the pattern of forest land loss is similar for all regions; the exception being the Pacific Coast where A2 predicts higher forest loss than A1B, but the difference is quite small (Wear 2011). Moreover, public forest and rangeland are expected to remain relatively static over the projection period.

FIGURE 5.

Projected change in U.S. forest land by region, 2010 to 2060, under a future of high economic growth and moderate population growth (A1B); no land-use change was assumed to occur on Federal land, and uses were held constant for water area, enrolled Conservation Reserve Program lands, and utility corridors for fuels, water, and electricity (source: 2010 Resources Planning Act assessment).

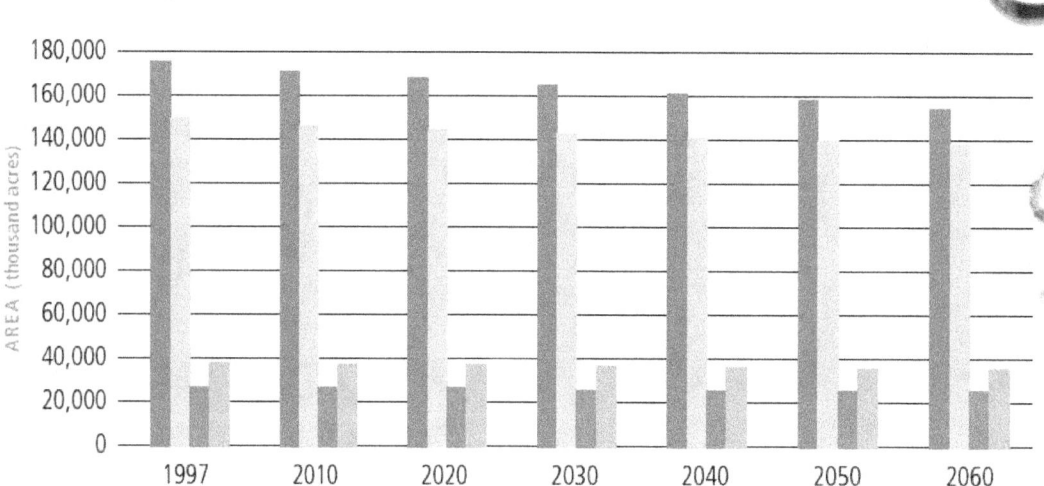

- South
- North
- Rocky Mountain
- Pacific Coast

After private forest land, cropland is expected to lose the most acreage, mostly in the Eastern United States, which currently has more cropland than the Western States. Cropland losses are nearly equally split between the North and South (Wear 2011). Rangeland losses are concentrated in the Rocky Mountains, which has about half the total rangeland losses. The remainder of rangeland losses is split between the South (primarily in Texas) and the Pacific Coast (mostly southern California).

Few large-scale studies have been conducted to relate climate to outdoor recreation, but an underlying assumption of this report is that long-term climate changes can affect recreation demand. Each storyline from the Intergovernmental Panel on Climate Change had multiple associated climate projections, which varied in response to the associated levels of greenhouse gas emissions. They also varied because of differences in the general circulation models that were associated with them in the RPA assessment (Joyce et al., in press).

The Intergovernmental Panel on Climate Change climate projections first were downscaled to the approximately 10-km scale and then aggregated to the county scale (Joyce et al., in press). At the scale of the contiguous United States, the average annual temperatures and total annual precipitation under A1B represent the warmest and the driest climate at 2060 (Fig. 6). Within A1B, the CGCM3.1 reflects the coolest (plus 2.55 °C) and wettest (plus 62.32 mm) climate over the projection period, and MIROC3.2 reflects the warmest (plus 4.21 °C) and driest (minus 107.39 mm); intermediate to them is CSIROMK3.5 with moderate temperature (plus 2.73 °C) and precipitation (plus 37.54 mm) changes. Although all areas of the United States show increases in temperature, the rates of change among regions vary somewhat, and regional differences in precipitation projections vary considerably (Joyce et al., in press).

FIGURE 6

U.S. temperature and precipitation changes from 1961 to 1990 (historical period) to the decade surrounding the year 2060 (2055 to 2064) under a future of high economic growth and moderate population growth (A1B) and climate scenarios predicted by three general circulation models of climate change: CGCM3.1, CSIROMK3.5, and MIROC3.2. (source: 2010 Resources Planning Act assessment).

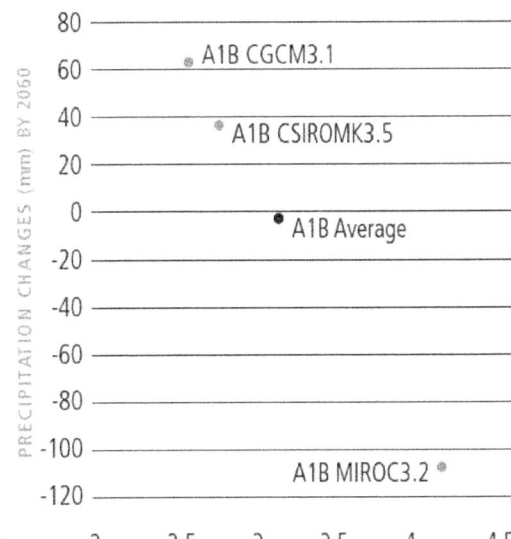

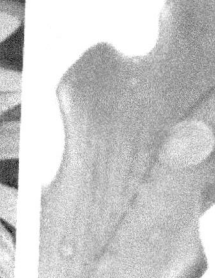

The purpose of this report is to evaluate how changes in population, demographics, economic conditions, land use, and climate likely will affect participants and days of participation in the North for 17 natural resource-based recreation activities. The demographic, climate, and land use projections described above were used to develop projections of future resource uses and conditions. Not all of the projected variables were used in all models, but all of the projection models used some subset of these variables. As a result, the projections and their underlying assumptions provide a common framework for comparing results across three climate futures associated with A1B.

This report proceeds in three main parts. First, we present the statistical methods and previous research that underlie regional per capita participation and consumption models. Next, we describe the data used in the estimation step, including projections of the various income and population growth factors and relevant assumptions—and we present estimation and simulation steps for regional participation and days projections by activity and climate future for A1B to 2060. Finally, we discuss some of the key findings within and across categories, and in association with the factors that are likely to drive change over the projection period.

Methods and Data

Models used to assess recreation demand decisions can be grouped into three basic categories: (1) site-specific user models, (2) site-specific aggregate models, and (3) population-level models. Cicchetti (1973) pioneered cross-sectional population-level models with the household-based 1965 National Survey of Recreation, which estimated annual participation and use nationally for many outdoor recreation activities; then used estimated models and Census Bureau projections of sociodemographic variables and population to forecast participation and use to 2000. Researchers have used the cross-sectional population-level approach to estimate and project participation and use for recreation activities at national and regional levels (Bowker 2001; Bowker et al., in press; Hof and Kaiser 1983a; Leeworthy et al. 2005; Walsh et al. 1992) and for previous RPA assessments (Bowker et al. 1999, Bowker et al. 2012, Hof and Kaiser 1983b). Researchers also have used alternative approaches—combining population data with individual site-level data or county-level data—to project national or regional recreation demand (Bowker et al. 2006, Cordell and Bergstrom 1991, Cordell et al. 1990, Englin and Shonkwiler 1995, English et al. 1993, Poudyal et al. 2008).

A major drawback of cross-sectional models, imposed by the nature of the data, is that the structure of the estimated models remains constant over the forecast period.

For example, the factors that influence participation or use are assumed to have the same effects throughout the projection period. Hence, with model parameters constant in time and barring major shifts in demographics, the results often are driven by population growth. This assumption can be tenuous. One consequence is that new sports brought about by technological changes or shifts in tastes and preferences (such as mountain biking, jet skiing, snowboarding, flat-water kayaking, and orienteering) are less likely to be correctly represented in the models. Moreover, if data are collected while activities are in a new or rapid growth phase, recent trends can be misleading; for example, although Cordell (2012) reported a recent increase in kayaking participation of 154 percent in less than a decade, sustaining such a rate of growth for 50 years would be unlikely. A further drawback of these models is the difficulty of accounting for the dampening effects of future congestion, supply limitations, economic downturns or upswings, and relative price changes on growth in participation and use. Nevertheless, without appropriate time-series data or panel data, researchers are left with the inherent limitations of cross-sectional models, as a second-best alternative to estimate and forecast participation and use.

Regional cross-sectional population-level logistic models were used to describe the probability of adult participation in each of the 17 activities as:

$$P_i = \frac{1}{[1+\exp(-X_i B_i)]} \qquad \text{(eq. 1)}$$

where

P_i = the probability that an individual participated in recreation activity i in the preceding year

X_i = a vector that contains sociodemographic characteristics unique to activity i across individuals, relevant supply variables for activity i across individual locations (Table 3), and at least one climate variable related to conditions at or near the individual's residence

B_i = a vector of parameters associated with activity i

Data were manipulated using SAS 9.1 (2004) and models were estimated using NLOGIT 4.0 (Greene 2009).

Logistic models for each activity, based on NSRE data from 1999 to 2008 (U.S. Department of Agriculture Forest Service 2009), were combined with 2008 baseline population-weighted sample averages for the explanatory variables to create an initial predicted per capita participation rate for each activity. The per capita participation rates were recalculated at 10-year intervals using projected changes in the explanatory variables. Indices then were created for the participation rates by which the NSRE 2005 to 2009 average population-weighted participation frequencies (Table 1) were scaled, leading to indexed per capita participation rates for each of the 17 activities.

We opted to index the NSRE averages by changes in model-predicted rates because doing so mitigates the potential for nonlinearity biases that are associated with complete reliance on logistic predicted values (Souter and Bowker 1996). The indexed participation rate estimates then were combined with projected changes in population, according to each of the three 2010 RPA assessment scenarios, to yield indexed values for total adult participants in the region across the 17 activities.

Participation intensity or consumption models were similar to the participation models listed above except that an integer metric represented use—the number of times, days, visits, trips, or events was modeled rather than the binary (yes/no) decision to participate. The general specification for the population-level consumption model was:

$$Y_i = f(X_i, Q_i) + u_i \qquad \text{(eq. 2)}$$

where

Y_i = the annual number of different days during which an individual participates in activity i

X_i = a vector of individual sociodemographic characteristics

Q_i = a vector of supply relevant variables for activity i

u_i = a random disturbance term specific to activity i

These integer or count data models are often estimated using negative binomial specifications with a link function of semi-logarithmic form (Bowker 2001, Bowker et al. 1999, Zawacki et al. 2000).

Variations of these consumption/demand models have been developed for onsite applications, where all observed visits were recorded as positive integers (Bowker and Leeworthy 1998). Such zero-truncated models have been applied extensively in onsite recreation demand estimation and valuation research (Bowker et al. 2007, Englin and Shonkwiler 1995, Hagerty and Moeltner 2005, Ovaskainen et al. 2001). In some studies, the estimated models have been extrapolated to general populations, assuming that visitors and nonvisitors come from the same general population of users (Englin and Shonkwiler 1995). This approach, wherein population data are combined with individual site-level data, was suggested by Cordell and Bergstrom (1991) and used in a previous RPA assessment by Cordell et al. (1990) with linear models to estimate outdoor recreation trips for 31 activities and to project the number of trips by activity from 1989 to 2040. English et al. (1993) extended the RPA models and projections to the regional level by combining parameter estimates from national models with regional explanatory variable values. Among others, Hagerty and Moeltner (2005) question the efficacy of extrapolating parameter estimates from the onsite demand models to the population at large.

Table 3—Socioeconomic and supply variables for modeling and forecasting outdoor recreation participation and days-of-participation by American adults.

Variable	Description
Gender	1=Male, 0=otherwise
American Indian	1=American Indian, 0=otherwise
Asian/Pacific Islander	1=Asian/Pacific Islander, 0=otherwise
Hispanic	1=Hispanic, 0=otherwise
Black	1=African American, 0=otherwise
Bachelors	1=Bachelor degree, 0=otherwise
Below High School	1=Less than high school, 0=otherwise
Post Graduate	1=Post-graduate degree, 0=otherwise
Some College	1=Some college or technical school, 0=otherwise
Age	Respondent age in years
Age Squared	Respondent age squared
Income	Respondent household income (2007 dollars)
Population Density	County area divided by population (base 1997)
Coastal	1=County on coast, 0=otherwise
For_ran_pcap	Sum of forest land acres and rangeland acres divided by population at county level and at 50, 100, 200-mile radii (base 1997)
Water_pcap	Water acres divided by population at county level and at 50, 100, 200-mile radii (base 1997)
Mtns_pcap	Mountainous acres divided by population (base 1997)
Pct_mtns_pcap	Percentage of county acres in mountains divided by population multiplied by 100000 (base 1997)
Natpark_pcap	Number of nature parks and similar institutions divided by population multiplied by 100000 (base 1997)
Fed_land_pcap	Sum U.S. Forest Service, National Park Service, U.S. Fish and Wildlife Service, Bureau of Land Management, U.S. Bureau of Reclamation, Tennessee Valley Authority, and U.S. Army Corps of Engineers acreage divided by population (base 1997)
Avg_elev	Average elevation in meters at county level and 50-, 100-, 200-mile radii (base 1997)

Household data, such as from the NSRE, may report zero visits; doing so eliminates problems related to onsite samples and extrapolating onsite models to general populations. In a previous RPA assessment analysis, Bowker et al. (1999) used data from the 1994 to 1995 NSRE, the U.S. Census, and the 1997 Forest Service National Outdoor Recreation Supply Information System database to project of participation and consumption (annual days and trips) for more than 20 natural resource-based outdoor activities, both nationally and in four geographical regions of the United States, from 2000 to 2050. That analysis moved beyond participation modeling to include negative binomial count models to estimate consumption (days and trips annually) and to project these measures over the same time period. Bowker (2001) followed the same approach, using NSRE and State-level data in projections from 2000 to 2020 of outdoor-recreation participation and consumption in Alaska. Leeworthy et al. (2005) used NSRE 2000 data in projecting participation and consumption of marine-related outdoor recreation through 2010. Bowker et al. (2006) applied similar methods with 2000 NSRE and National Visitor Use Monitoring data (English et al. 2002, U.S. Department of Agriculture Forest Service 2010) in developing projections of wilderness and primitive area recreation participation and consumption from 2002 through 2050.

Alternatively, if one suspects that observed zeros for the dependent variable (days of participation) are excessive or not entirely caused by the same data generating process as the positive values, using a hurdle model structure or a zero-inflated count procedure would be appropriate (Cameron and Trivedi 1998). The hurdle model that we employed combines the probability of participation (threshold) with the estimated number of days for those participating, as shown below.

$$E[Y|X] = Pr[Y > 0|X1] * E_{y>0}[Y|Y > 0, X2] \qquad (eq. 3)$$

where

E = expected value operator

Pr = probability of participation

Y = days of participation

X = vector of explanatory variables.

The hurdle model allowed different vectors of explanatory variables ($X1$ and $X2$), and thus parameters, for the respective products of the expectation in eq. 3—probability and conditional-days portions of the model—with probability estimated as a logistic (eq. 1) and conditional days estimated as a truncated negative binomial, thus leading to two unique sets of estimated parameters. Each of the 17 regional outdoor recreation activity day hurdle models were estimated with NLOGIT 4.0 (Greene 2009), using 1999 to 2009 NSRE data for U.S. households (U.S. Department of Agriculture Forest Service 2009), county-level climate data (Joyce et al., in press), county-level land use data (Wear 2011), and recreation supply data (Cordell et al. 2012). Although we did not formally test the hurdle model against the simpler untruncated negative binomial model (Bowker et al. 1999) for each activity, the parameter estimates and the significant variables for the logistic portion nearly always differed from the conditional days portion, thus validating the choice of the hurdle model.

As in the procedure for the participation models and indices, hurdle model parameter estimates were combined with 2008 NSRE baseline participation and days estimates (Table 1), projected explanatory variables, and projected population changes under each of the climate scenarios to provide indices of annual days-of-participation growth projections for the activities listed in Table 1. The three climate scenarios (CGCM3.1, MIROC3.2, and CSIROMK3.5) were used in conjunction with A1B.

Table 3 lists socioeconomic and supply variables for the various models and projections. The preponderance of these variables was included in the NSRE database (U.S. Department of Agriculture Forest Service 2009). Additional variables related to supply were obtained from Cordell et al. (2013). Projections of land use change variables were obtained from Wear (2011). Historical as well as projected climate data were obtained from Joyce et al. (in press). As little or no literature was available to link climate with household participation and consumption of recreation activities, an ad hoc approach was followed during the model estimation stage, wherein climate variables were created based on 6-year moving averages and arbitrary distances from county centroids. Table 4 lists representative climate variables. Each estimated model was limited to one climate variable; selection occurred on an ad hoc basis, primarily based on model fit.

Table 4—Climate variables used for estimating and forecasting outdoor recreation participation and days-of-participation by American adults.

Variable	Description
Ppt_monthly_average_d100[a]	Daily average of precipitation for all months for resident county and counties within 100 miles of resident county centroid
Ppt_monthly_average_d200	Daily average of precipitation for all months for resident county and counties within 200 miles of resident county centroid
Spring_PET_d200	Spring average daily potential evapotranspiration for resident county and counties within 200 miles of resident county centroid
Tmax_fall_d50	Average monthly maximum fall temperature for resident county and counties within 50 miles of resident county centroid
Tmax_geq_25_d200	Percentage of month where average monthly maximum temperature exceeded 25 degrees Celsius for resident county and counties within 200 miles of resident county centroid
Tmax_geq_35	Percentage of months where average monthly maximum temperature exceeded 35 degrees Celsius in the resident county
Tmax_geq35_d100	Percentage of month where average monthly maximum temperature exceeded 35 degrees Celsius for resident county and counties within 100 miles of resident county centroid
Tmax_geq35_d200	Percentage of month where average monthly maximum temperature exceeded 35 degrees Celsius for resident county and counties within 200 miles of resident county centroid
Tmax_spring	Average of the average monthly maximum temperature in spring in the resident county
Tmax_spring_d100	Average of the average monthly maximum temperature in spring for the resident county and counties within 100 miles of resident county centroid
Tmax_summer	Average of the average monthly maximum temperature in summer in the resident county
Tmax_summer_d50	Average of the average monthly maximum temperature in summer for the resident county and counties within 50 miles of resident county centroid
Tmax_summer_d100	Average of the average monthly maximum temperature in summer for the resident county and counties within 100 miles of resident county centroid
Tmax_summer_d200	Average of the average monthly maximum temperature in summer for the resident county and counties within 200 miles of resident county centroid
Tmax_winter	Average of the average monthly maximum temperature in winter in the resident county
Tmax_winter_d100	Average of the average monthly maximum temperature in winter for the resident county and counties within 100 miles of resident county centroid
Tmin_leq_0	Percent of month where average monthly minimum temperature was below 0 degrees Celsius in the resident county
Tmin_leq_neg10	Percent of month where average monthly minimum temperature was below -10 degrees Celsius in the resident county

Table 4 continued

Variable	Description
Total_ppt_d100	Monthly average of total monthly precipitation in resident county and counties within 100 miles of resident county centroid
Total_ppt_d200	Monthly average of total monthly precipitation in resident county and counties within 200 miles of resident county centroid
Winter_PET_d50	Average of average daily potential evapotranspiration in winter for resident county and counties within 50 miles of resident county centroid
Winter_PET_d200	Average of average daily potential evapotranspiration in winter for resident county and counties within 200 miles of resident county centroid
Yearly_PET_d200	Average of average daily potential evapotranspiration for resident county and counties within 200 miles of resident county centroid

[a]*All averages are calculated over 6-year periods, for example, historic data are based on 2001 to 2006 data, 2060 projections are based on averages from 2055 to 2060. Seasons were divided into 3-month periods based on the following categories: winter (December, January, and February), spring (March, April, and May), summer (June, July, and August), and fall (September, October, and November).*

Results

As discussed in the previous section, results were estimated for 17 outdoor recreation participation models (eq. 1). All models included socioeconomic variables, in addition to at least one variable reflecting land use change or relative supply of settings typically associated with the particular activity. The estimated equations are reported in the Appendix (found on the CD included with this report). In addition, each model included one climate variable (Table 5). Reported results include parameter estimates for each activity, values for explanatory variables by scenario and year, odds ratios which indicate the probability of participation occurring in one group compared to the probability of it occurring in another group, fit statistics, and graphics of total participant growth by activity and climate scenario.

Logistic parameter estimates then were combined with available projections of relevant explanatory variables under the updated A1B storyline (high economic growth, moderate population growth), including one associated with each of the three climate scenarios—the coolest and wettest CGCM3.1, the warmest and driest MIROC3.2, and the intermediate CSIROMK3.5—to create indexed per capita participation estimates at 10-year intervals through 2060. These indices were, in turn, combined with population projections for A1B to develop estimated participant indices.

The participant indices then were applied to a beginning baseline estimate of participants for each activity (based on weighted regional averages calculated from 2005 to 2009 NSRE data) to yield the projected number of adult participants. The 4-year average around 2008 was chosen to avoid any abnormality associated with a single year.

The hurdle model (eq. 3) combined the probability of participation in an activity with the expected value of days participating, given that the individual actually participated. The estimated logistic models were thus combined with conditional participation days models to complete the hurdle model. Given that only those who participated were included in the conditional days portion of the model (thus ensuring no zero observations for days), a truncated negative binomial model was employed for estimation. As with the logistic participation models above, days models were estimated for each of the 17 outdoor recreation activities reported in Table 1. Table 5 lists climate variables used in the days models.

Table 5—Climate variables used for estimating and forecasting outdoor recreation participation and days-of-participation.

Recreation activity	Model	Climate variable
Developed site use	Participation Days	Summer_PET_d200 Spring_PET
Interpretive site use	Participation Days	Total_ppt_d100 Fall_PET
Birding	Participation Days	Spring_PET_d200 Total_ppt_d50
Nature viewing	Participation Days	Summer_PET_d200 Total_ppt_d50
Challenge	Participation Days	Total_ppt Total_ppt_d50
Equestrian	Participation Days	Summer_PET_d200 Tmin_fall
Day hiking	Participation Days	Winter_PET_d200 Total_ppt_d50
Primitive area use	Participation Days	Fall_PET_d200 Summer_PET_d50
Off-road driving	Participation Days	Tmax_fall_d200 Total_ppt_d200
Motorized water	Participation Days	Summer_PET_d50 Total_ppt_d200
Motorized snow	Participation Days	Winter_PET_d200 Total_ppt_d100
Hunting	Participation Days	Fall_PET_d100 Tmax_geq_25_d100
Fishing	Participation Days	Summer_PET_d100 Summer_PET_d200
Developed skiing	Participation Days	Total_ppt Spring_PET_d200
Undeveloped skiing	Participation Days	Tmax_winter_d200 Tmax_winter_d200
Swimming	Participation Days	Tmax_summer_d200 Tmax_geq_25_d200
Floating	Participation Days	Summer_PET_d200 Spring_PET_d200

Total days for each activity were estimated following a procedure similar to that for estimating participants. First, days of participation per participant were nonlinearly regressed on relevant explanatory variables including at least one climate variable. Parameter estimates from the respective negative binomial models then were combined with projected explanatory variables under A1B and associated climate model forecasts, at 10-year intervals, to create indexed per capita days of participation, which were combined with population projections for A1B to develop estimated per participant days indices. These indices then were applied to a beginning baseline estimate of participation days for each activity, based on weighted national averages calculated from the 2005 to 2009 NSRE data, to yield projections of total adult activity days. As with the participant estimates, a 4-year average around 2008 was chosen to avoid any aberrations associated with a single year. The results of participation and days-of-participation models are shown in the series of tables that follow. In addition to results simulated under each climate scenario associated with A1B, an average across the climate scenarios is also reported.

Visiting developed sites—Activities associated with this composite activity include family gathering, picnicking, and developed camping. Per capita participation for this activity is currently high and projected to remain relatively constant into the future, decreasing slightly on average, across climate scenarios (Table 6). The minor decrease in adult participation rate, coupled with population growth, suggests an increase in users of 27 to 35 percent by 2060, or about 24 million more per year than the current 80.5 million.

Average annual days per developed site visitor are projected to decrease by 10 percent on average across climate scenarios, or just over 1 day per participant per year. CSIRO and MIROC climate forecasts roughly doubled the decrease from the CGCM model (Table 6). Total days of developed use increase 12 to 27 percent across the climate scenarios. Given the relatively small changes in average days of developed site visitation per participant across the climate scenarios, the key driver in the increase in total days for this activity is likely to be population growth. Across all climate scenarios, the average expected increase in annual days of developed site visitation is about 17 percent or 160 million days for the region annually by 2060.

Table 6—Projected developed site visit participation and use (family gathering, picnicking, developed camping) by adults in the Northern United States, 2008 to 2060, under Resources Planning Act (RPA) scenario A1B and related climate futures.

RPA Scenario	2008	2060 Climate Average[a]	2060 Climate Average[a]	2060 CGCM3.1	2060 CSIRO-MK3.5	2060 MIROC3.2
	Per capita participation		Percent increase (decrease) from 2008			
A1B	0.825	0.791	(4)[b]	0	(6)	(6)
	Adult participants (millions)		Percent increase (decrease) from 2008			
A1B	80.5	104.2	30	35	27	27
	Days per participant		Percent increase (decrease) from 2008			
A1B	11.69	10.58	(10)	(5)	(11)	(12)
	Total days (millions)		Percent increase (decrease) from 2008			
A1B	943.3	1,106.2	17	27	13	12

[a]Result of average across CGCM3.1, CSIROMK3.5, and MIROC3.2.

[b]Parentheses denotes decrease.

Visiting interpretive areas—Interpretive areas include nature centers, zoos, historic sites, and prehistoric sites. More than 67 million adults, or about 69 percent of all residents in the region, participated in at least one activity in this category annually from 2005 to 2009. The projections indicate participation rates are likely to be stable at about 9 percent across climate scenarios (Table 7). Climate effects are expected to result in small differences in participation rates, offset by consistently higher numbers of days per participant (up to half a day per year on average). As per capita participation is expected to rise 9 percent,

the number of participants will likely exceed the rate of population growth. The higher growth in participation rate for this activity group compared to visiting developed sites has several possible causes—visiting developed sites is negatively related to age, which is expected to rise by 2060, and positively related to available Federal land per capita—that are less important in interpretive site visitation, as is climate change. Total annual days of interpretive site visits is projected to increase by two-thirds, on average, or by 343 million days per year by 2060.

Table 7—Projected interpretive site visit participation and use (visiting natural sites, prehistoric, or historic sites) by adults in the Northern United States, 2008 to 2060, under Resources Planning Act (RPA) scenario A1B and related climate futures.

			Year			
RPA Scenario	2008	2060 Climate Average[a]	2060 Climate Average[a]	2060 CGCM3.1	2060 CSIRO-MK3.5	2060 MIROC3.2
	Per capita participation		Percent increase (decrease) from 2008			
A1B	0.686	0.747	9	9	9	9
	Adult participants (millions)		Percent increase (decrease) from 2008			
A1B	67.0	98.5	47	47	48	47
	Days per participant		Percent increase (decrease) from 2008			
A1B	7.69	8.70	13	8	14	17
	Total days (millions)		Percent increase (decrease) from 2008			
A1B	516.0	858.5	66	59	68	72

[a]Result of average across CGCM3.1, CSIROMK3.5, and MIROC3.2.

This category includes birding, both viewing and photographing; it also includes the more general activity aggregate called viewing, which consists of any activities that involve the viewing, photography, or study of natural settings, or the noncommercial gathering of plants or animals. From 2005 to 2009, an average of 38 percent of northern adults, or 37 million people, participated annually in birding. In the more broadly defined viewing aggregate, which would include birding, nearly 82 percent of the adult population, or about 79 million people, participated annually.

Birding—Participation in birding is expected to remain stable over the next 50 years, with the participation rate declining by about 1.4 percent to about 37 percent of northern adults. Coupling this decrease with the population growth expected under A1B would mean a regional increase in birders of 24 to 40 percent, depending on the climate scenario (Table 8). On average, the expected annual increase is 30 percent, or about 11 million adults in 2060. The number of days per participant is expected to decrease uniformly (4 percent) across the three climate scenarios. Given that adult birders in the region averaged nearly 100 days per year

Table 8—Projected birding participation and use (viewing or photographing birds) by adults in the Northern United States, 2008 to 2060, under Resources Planning Act (RPA) scenario A1B and related climate futures.

RPA Scenario	2008	2060 Climate Average[a]	2060 Climate Average[a]	2060 CGCM3.1	2060 CSIRO-MK3.5	2060 MIROC3.2
	Per capita participation		Percent increase (decrease) from 2008			
A1B	0.382	0.368	(4)[b]	3	(7)	(8)
	Adult participants (millions)		Percent increase (decrease) from 2008			
A1B	37.2	48.3	30	40	26	24
	Days per participant		Percent increase (decrease) from 2008			
A1B	99.8	96.1	(4)	(3)	(4)	(4)
	Total days (millions)		Percent increase (decrease) from 2008			
A1B	3,696	4,625	25	35	21	19

[a]Result of average across CGCM3.1, CSIROMK3.5, and MIROC3.2.

[b]Parentheses denotes decrease.

from 2005 to 2009, an annual decrease of 4 days would not have much of an effect on the annual totals, which should increase by 19 to 35 percent over the 50-year period. The largest increase, 1,310 million days per year, would occur under CGM3.1, which is marginally wetter and cooler than the other two scenarios at the national level.

Viewing—The regional adult participation rate in the broader viewing category will likely remain essentially unchanged over the next 50 years, suggesting that viewing participants will increase at about the rate of population increase. By 2060, the total number of nature viewers per year is expected to increase by 35 percent to about 107 million adults (Table 9).

Annual average nature viewing days per participant will likely decrease across all scenarios by 8 to 10 percent, or about 2 weeks per year, resulting in one of the largest relative decreases in total days per participant across all activities (Table 9). The decrease in viewing days per participant appears to be driven by a number of factors, among them, projected increases in total population density and in minority populations, and a projected decrease in public land per capita in the region. Despite the predicted decrease in annual days per participant, total viewing days will likely increase, driven by the increase in the number of participants, by an average of about 3,104 million days per year by 2060.

Table 9—Projected nature viewing participation and use (viewing, photography, study, or nature gathering related to fauna, flora, or natural settings) by adults in the Northern United States, 2008 to 2060, under Resources Planning Act (RPA) scenario A1B and related climate futures.

RPA Scenario	2008	2060 Climate Average[a]	2060 Climate Average[a]	2060 CGCM3.1	2060 CSIRO-MK3.5	2060 MIROC3.2
	Per capita participation		Percent increase (decrease) from 2008			
A1B	0.815	0.813	0	3	(2)[b]	(2)
	Adult participants (millions)		Percent increase (decrease) from 2008			
A1B	79.5	107.0	35	39	32	33
	Days per participant		Percent increase (decrease) from 2008			
A1B	175.7	159.5	(9)	(8)	(10)	(9)
	Total days (millions)		Percent increase (decrease) from 2008			
A1B	13,925	17,029	22	27	19	21

[a]Result of average across CGCM3.1, CSIROMK3.5, and MIROC3.2.

[b]Parentheses denotes decrease.

Table 10—Projected challenge activity participation and use (mountain climbing, rock climbing, caving) by adults in the Northern United States, 2008 to 2060, under Resources Planning Act (RPA) scenario A1B and related climate futures.

			Year			
RPA Scenario	2008	2060 Climate Average[a]	2060 Climate Average[a]	2060 CGCM3.1	2060 CSIRO-MK3.5	2060 MIROC3.2
	Per capita participation		Percent increase (decrease) from 2008			
A1B	0.095	0.086	(10)[b]	(6)	(14)	(9)
	Adult participants (millions)		Percent increase (decrease) from 2008			
A1B	9.4	11.4	22	27	16	22
	Days per participant		Percent increase (decrease) from 2008			
A1B	3.89	3.82	(2)	0	(4)	(2)
	Total days (millions)		Percent increase (decrease) from 2008			
A1B	37.7	45.1	20	27	12	21

[a] Result of average across CGCM3.1. CSIROMK3.5. and MIROC3.2.

[b] Parentheses denotes decrease.

BACKCOUNTRY ACTIVITIES

Backcountry activities are most often pursued in undeveloped but accessible lands. The category includes these four activities, or activity composites: (1) challenge activities, (2) horseback riding, (3) hiking, and (4) visiting primitive areas.

Challenge activities—Challenge activities, often associated with young and affluent adults, include caving, mountain biking, mountain climbing, and rock climbing. Nearly 10 percent of adults in the region currently engage in these activities, a rate expected to decrease by about 10 percent in 50 years (Table 10).

Population growth in the region will likely offset expected participation-rate decreases, leading to increases in the number of participants of 16 to 27 percent across the climate scenarios. Participation is projected to grow by 22 percent on average, or by about 2 million adults per year through 2060. The number of days per participant will be almost unchanged across climate scenarios, remaining at less than 4 days per year among participants. Coupled with population growth rates, total days of challenge sport participation will likely increase 12 to 27 percent annually by 2060. On average this increase would result in an additional 7.4 million days of activity per year.

Table 11—Projected equestrian participation and use (horseback riding on trails) by adults in the Northern United States, 2008 to 2060, under Resources Planning Act (RPA) scenario A1B and related climate futures.

RPA Scenario	2008	2060 Climate Average[a]	2060 Climate Average[a]	2060 CGCM3.1	2060 CSIRO-MK3.5	2060 MIROC3.2
	Per capita participation		Percent increase (decrease) from 2008			
A1B	0.059	0.084	42	23	54	48
	Adult participants (millions)		Percent increase (decrease) from 2008			
A1B	5.77	11.05	91	67	108	100
	Days per participant		Percent increase (decrease) from 2008			
A1B	12.63	12.16	(4)[b]	(1)	(4)	(7)
	Total days (millions)		Percent increase (decrease) from 2008			
A1B	72.3	133.0	84	65	100	87

[a] Result of average across CGCM3.1, CSIROMK3.5, and MIROC3.2.

[b] Parentheses denotes decrease.

Horseback riding—Horseback riding on trails claimed 6 percent of the northern adult population annually as participants in 2008—a percentage expected to increase to more than 8 percent by 2060, with the biggest increases occurring under the warmer and drier climate scenarios predicted by CSIROMK3.5 and MIROC3.2 (Table 11). When population growth is included to derive the number of annual participants, the expected average increase across the three climate scenarios is 91 percent, or just about twice the 5.8 million 2008 participants. Relative to previously discussed activities—such as visiting developed sites, nature viewing, and challenge sports—expected changes in climate do not appear to have a dampening effect on horseback-riding participation. The per capita number of days of participation would remain about constant over the projection period, dropping about a half day per year, or 4 percent on average. However, factoring in population growth would lead to increases in the total days of horseback riding of 65 to 100 percent by 2060, depending on the climate scenario, with the average increase expected to be about 61 million days per year.

Table 12—Projected day hiking participation and use by adults in the Northern United States, 2008 to 2060, under Resources Planning Act (RPA) scenario A1B and related climate futures.

RPA Scenario	2008	2060 Climate Average[a]	2060 Climate Average[a]	2060 CGCM3.1	2060 CSIRO-MK3.5	2060 MIROC3.2
	Per capita participation		Percent increase (decrease) from 2008			
A1B	0.327	0.319	(2)[b]	0	(5)	(2)
	Adult participants (millions)		Percent increase (decrease) from 2008			
A1B	32.4	42.7	32	35	28	32
	Days per participant		Percent increase (decrease) from 2008			
A1B	22.44	20.86	(7)	(6)	(9)	(7)
	Total days (millions)		Percent increase (decrease) from 2008			
A1B	723.8	886.0	22	28	17	23

[a]Result of average across CGCM3.1, CSIROMK3.5, and MIROC3.2.

[b]Parentheses denotes decrease.

Day hiking—Hiking is the most popular single backcountry activity with about a third of all northern adults, or about 32.4 million people, hiking in 2008. Among the three climate scenarios, hiking participation per capita is expected to remain about constant out to 2060 (Table 12). Thus, with population growth, hikers in the region should increase by about a third in 2060. Hiking is the only activity in which Hispanics demonstrated a higher participation rate than Caucasians (Appendix). Annual days of hiking per participant are forecasted to decrease evenly across the climate scenarios, averaging 7 percent or about 1.6 days per year.

Thus, total annual days of hiking will likely increase less than population growth, but the result would nevertheless be an increase in hiking days of approximately 162 million days by 2060.

Visiting primitive areas—The final backcountry activity, an aggregate called visiting primitive areas, consists of backpacking, primitive camping, and visiting a designated or undesignated wilderness. This composite accounted for 36.1 million regional participants in 2008, or about 37 percent of all adults. Annual per capita participation in this category is expected to decrease 10 to 34 percent over the next 50 years across the climate scenarios, an average 8.5-percent drop (Table 13). Increased population density, declining Federal land area per capita, and increasing population diversity appear to be factors influencing the participation rate decrease (Appendix). However, overall participation is expected to increase by an average of 4 percent, to under 38 million adults by 2060, because population growth offsets the decrease in participation rates.

Average annual days per participant visiting primitive areas is projected to decrease 14 to 26 percent across climate scenarios (Table 13), to more than 2 days per year by 2060. The decrease in participation rate and the drop in average participant days per year would lead to annual average decreases of 18 percent, from the current 415 million to 342 million days per year. However, the climate scenario showing the smallest change from the 2008 baseline, CGCM3.1, predicts a 5-percent annual increase in visitation days to less than or equal to 436 million by 2060.

Table 13—Projected primitive area visit participation and use (backpacking, primitive camping, wilderness) by adults in the Northern United States, 2008 to 2060, under Resources Planning Act (RPA) scenario A1B and related climate futures.

RPA Scenario	2008	2060 Climate Average[a]	2060 Climate Average[a]	2060 CGCM3.1	2060 CSIRO-MK3.5	2060 MIROC3.2
	Per capita participation		Percent increase (decrease) from 2008			
A1B	0.367	0.282	(23)[b]	(10)	(26)	(34)
	Adult participants (millions)		Percent increase (decrease) from 2008			
A1B	36.1	37.4	4	22	0	(11)
	Days per participant		Percent increase (decrease) from 2008			
A1B	11.42	9.01	(21)	(14)	(26)	(24)
	Total days (millions)		Percent increase (decrease) from 2008			
A1B	415	342.0	(18)	5	(26)	(32)

[a] Result of average across CGCM3.1, CSIROMK3.5, and MIROC3.2.

[b] Parentheses denotes decrease.

Three categories of motorized activities were considered: off-road driving, motorized water use, and snow use.

Off-road driving— Participation in off-road driving averaged about 18 percent of the northern adult population, or about 17.3 million adults, annually from 2005 to 2009 (Table 14). Future participation rates are expected to decrease by 4 to 13 percent, depending on the climate scenarios. Among factors leading to the decrease are the expected increase in minority populations and general aging of the total population (Appendix). Despite these declining rates of growth in per capita participation, the number of participants in off-road driving will likely increase 18 to 29 percent under the climate scenarios to somewhere between 20 and 22 million people in 2060, because the rate of population growth is expected to outstrip any decrease in per capita participation.

Annual days of off-road driving per participant is projected to decrease 11 to 14 percent, or about 2 days per year by 2060 (Table 14) with only small variations among climate scenarios.

Table 14—Projected motorized off-road participation and use (off-road driving) by adults in the Northern United States, 2008 to 2060, under Resources Planning Act (RPA) scenario A1B and related climate futures.

		Year				
RPA Scenario	2008	2060 Climate Average[a]	2060 Climate Average[a]	2060 CGCM3.1	2060 CSIRO-MK3.5	2060 MIROC3.2
	Per capita participation		Percent increase (decrease) from 2008			
A1B	0.176	0.162	(8)[b]	(4)	(8)	(13)
	Adult participants (millions)		Percent increase (decrease) from 2008			
A1B	17.3	21.4	24	29	25	18
	Days per participant		Percent increase (decrease) from 2008			
A1B	16.43	14.36	(13)	(11)	(14)	(13)
	Total days (millions)		Percent increase (decrease) from 2008			
A1B	282.8	306.7	8	16	7	3

[a] Result of average across CGCM3.1, CSIROMK3.5, and MIROC3.2.

[b] Parentheses denotes decrease.

These decreases in participation rate and average annual days per participant imply that, under all scenarios, the total number of days of off-road driving will increase at a lower rate than respective population growth rates. Nevertheless, on average, the amount of total off-road driving days per year is expected to increase from 282.8 to more than 306 million days in the region.

Motorized snow use—Motorized snow use, or snowmobiling, is a geographically limited activity undertaken by more than 7 percent of northern residents in 2008. Per capita participation in snowmobiling is projected to decrease 58 to 78 percent under all climate scenarios (Table 15).

Regional changes in ethnicity, an aging population, declining Federal land per capita, and climate appear to be driving factors. Total snowmobiling participants are projected to decrease from 7 million in 2008 to between 2.1 and 3.9 million by 2060, depending on the climate scenario. Average annual days per participant would decrease by about 1 day per year on average. Coupled with the decrease in numbers of participants, this suggests a potential decrease in annual snowmobiling days of 52 to 74 percent by 2060. Averaged across the climate scenarios, the change implies a drop of annual snowmobiling days from 54.8 million in 2008 to 20.3 million in 2060.

Table 15—Projected motorized snow activity participation and use (snowmobiling) by adults in the Northern United States, 2008 to 2060, under Resources Planning Act (RPA) scenario A1B and related climate futures.

RPA Scenario	2008	2060 Climate Average[a]	2060 Climate Average[a]	2060 CGCM3.1	2060 CSIRO-MK3.5	2060 MIROC3.2
	Per capita participation		Percent increase (decrease) from 2008			
A1B	0.071	0.022	(69)[b]	(58)	(78)	(69)
	Adult participants (millions)		Percent increase (decrease) from 2008			
A1B	7.0	3.0	(58)	(44)	(70)	(59)
	Days per participant		Percent increase (decrease) from 2008			
A1B	7.87	6.89	(12)	(14)	(11)	(12)
	Total days (millions)		Percent increase (decrease) from 2008			
A1B	54.8	20.3	(63)	(52)	(74)	(64)

[a] Result of average across CGCM3.1, CSIROMK3.5, and MIROC3.2.

[b] Parentheses denotes decrease.

Table 16—Projected motorized water participation and use (motor boating, waterskiing, using personal watercraft) by adults in the Northern United States, 2008 to 2060, under Resources Planning Act (RPA) scenario A1B and related climate futures.

RPA Scenario	2008	2060 Climate Average[a]	2060 Climate Average[a]	2060 CGCM3.1	2060 CSIRO-MK3.5	2060 MIROC3.2
	Per capita participation		Percent increase (decrease) from 2008			
A1B	0.268	0.361	35	20	45	39
	Adult participants (millions)		Percent increase (decrease) from 2008			
A1B	26.1	47.3	82	61	96	88
	Days per participant		Percent increase (decrease) from 2008			
A1B	14.65	16.01	9	6	12	10
	Total days (millions)		Percent increase (decrease) from 2008			
A1B	378.8	752.8	99	72	118	106

[a]Result of average across CGCM3.1, CSIROMK3.5, and MIROC3.2.

Motorized water use—Motorized water activities involve motor boats, water skis, or personal watercraft. This combination of related activities had the highest per capita participation rate among motorized outdoor activities at 27 percent, or about 26.1 million adult participants, in 2008 (Table 16). Per capita participation is expected to grow by 20 to 45 percent over the next five decades to an average of 36 percent of all adults in the region. The highest growth rate is expected under the climate scenarios that are characterized by relatively higher average temperatures and less average rainfall. Overall, the numbers of adult participants in motorized water activities will likely increase faster than the population under all climate scenarios, for a total of 42 to 51 million participants in 2060.

Motorized water use participant days totaled about 378.8 million in 2008, or slightly less than 15 days annually per participant (Table 16). Days per participant are expected to increase 9 percent on average, or about 1.4 days per year by 2060. Combining population growth with increasing participation and annual days per participant would result in a 72- to 118-percent increase by 2060, meaning that, on average, the number of motorized water use days would double by 2060.

The traditional consumptive wildlife pursuits of hunting and fishing remain popular outdoor activities for northern adults, with about 11.3 million hunting and 28.7 million fishing participants in 2008. However, on a per capita basis, these pursuits have shown some decrease from past decades (Cordell 2012).

Hunting—Hunting is the legal pursuit of big game, small game, or migratory birds (as identified by an NSRE hunting screener question). The northern adult hunting participation rate, nearly 12 percent in 2008, is projected to decrease by 26 to 47 percent across climate scenarios by 2060 (Table 17)—with the pattern being that the bigger the change in climate conditions, the bigger the effect on hunting participation. The average decrease is projected to be 4 to 5 percentage points, meaning that about 7 percent of the adults will be hunting in 2060. The factors that appear to be associated with the drop in hunting participation are increased education levels, increased population density, diminishing availability of public land per capita, and increased minority populations (Appendix).

Partly offset by population growth, the projected number of hunting participants is expected to drop on average across climate alternatives by 16 percent to about 9.5 million hunters by 2060. Across all the climate scenarios, average annual days in the field per hunter is projected to decrease 13 to 20 percent, or a little more than 3 days per hunter per year (Table 17). Climate appears to have less effect on the average annual days a hunter spends in the field than on whether one participates in hunting. Total annual adult hunting days, estimated at about 209.6 million in 2008, is expected to decrease by an average of about 30 percent by 2060 to just below 146 million days per year.

Fishing—Fishing participation—which includes warmwater and coldwater fishing, saltwater fishing, and anadromous fishing—can be either consumptive or catch-and-release. Unlike hunting, the adult participation rate for fishing is expected to increase over the next five decades. Currently, 29.6 percent of northern adults claim to fish. This rate is expected to increase by 3 to 27 percent by 2060 (Table 18). On average, the warmer and drier climate change scenarios, CSIROMK3.5 and MIROC3.2, would result in larger increases in the participation rate than CGCM3.1. Coupled with population growth, the number of fishing participants is projected to rise by 39 to 71 percent by 2060. Averaged across climate scenarios, this implies an increase in annual anglers to about 45 million at the end of the projection period.

Table 17—Projected hunting participation and use (small game, big game, migratory bird, other) by adults in the Northern United States, 2008 to 2060, under Resources Planning Act (RPA) scenario A1B and related climate futures.

RPA Scenario	2008	2060 Climate Average[a]	2060 Climate Average[a]	2060 CGCM3.1	2060 CSIRO-MK3.5	2060 MIROC3.2
	Per capita participation		Percent increase (decrease) from 2008			
A1B	0.117	0.073	(38)[b]	(26)	(41)	(47)
	Adult participants (millions)		Percent increase (decrease) from 2008			
A1B	11.3	9.5	(16)	0	(20)	(28)
	Days per participant		Percent increase (decrease) from 2008			
A1B	18.84	15.53	(18)	(13)	(20)	(19)
	Total days (millions)		Percent increase (decrease) from 2008			
A1B	209.6	145.9	(30)	(12)	(36)	(42)

[a] Result of average across CGCM3.1, CSIROMK3.5, and MIROC3.2.

[b] Parentheses denotes decrease.

Table 18—Projected fishing participation and use (cold water, warm water, saltwater, anadromous) by adults in the Northern United States, 2008 to 2060, under Resources Planning Act (RPA) scenario A1B and related climate futures.

RPA Scenario	2008	2060 Climate Average[a]	2060 Climate Average[a]	2060 CGCM3.1	2060 CSIRO-MK3.5	2060 MIROC3.2
	Per capita participation		Percent increase (decrease) from 2008			
A1B	0.296	0.347	17	3	27	22
	Adult participants (millions)		Percent increase (decrease) from 2008			
A1B	28.7	45.4	58	39	71	65
	Days per participant		Percent increase (decrease) from 2008			
A1B	18.14	20.28	12	0	19	16
	Total days (millions)		Percent increase (decrease) from 2008			
A1B	515.7	919.3	78	39	104	91

[a] Result of average across CGCM3.1, CSIROMK3.5, and MIROC3.2.

Fishing days per participant are forecasted to increase up to 19 percent by 2060, or by about 2 days per year on average (Table 18). Overall, annual fishing days are expected to increase across all climate scenarios by 39 to 104 percent during the next five decades, with the warmer and drier scenarios seeing the largest increases. On average, this would mean an increase in annual fishing days for the region of 78 percent, or about 403.6 million days.

NON-MOTORIZED WINTER ACTIVITIES

Non-motorized winter activities include developed skiing (downhill skiing and snowboarding) and undeveloped skiing (cross-country skiing and snowshoeing).

Developed skiing—Developed skiing claimed an adult participation rate of 11.6 percent, about 11.6 million participants, annually from 2005 through 2009. Across the three climate scenarios, the participation rate for developed skiing is expected to increase by 25 to 32 percent or about 29 percent on average to about 15 percent of the adult population (Table 19). As with other income-dependent activities, the growth in household income associated with A1B would be a major driving factor in developed skiing participation rates, along with total precipitation, and education level increases (Appendix). The increases in participation rate, combined with population growth, suggest that the number of developed skiing participants could grow by about 8.5 million participants to over 20 million per year by 2060.

Table 19—Projected developed skiing participation and use (downhill skiing, snowboarding) by adults in the Northern United States, 2008 to 2060, under Resources Planning Act (RPA) scenario A1B and related climate futures.

RPA Scenario	2008	2060 Climate Average[a]	2060 Climate Average[a]	2060 CGCM3.1	2060 CSIRO-MK3.5	2060 MIROC3.2
	Per capita participation		Percent increase (decrease) from 2008			
A1B	0.116	0.149	29	32	25	29
	Adult participants (millions)		Percent increase (decrease) from 2008			
A1B	11.6	20.1	74	78	69	75
	Days per participant		Percent increase (decrease) from 2008			
A1B	6.99	4.75	(32)[b]	(22)	(37)	(37)
	Total days (millions)		Percent increase (decrease) from 2008			
A1B	81.3	96.3	18	39	6	9

[a]Result of average across CGCM3.1, CSIROMK3.5, and MIROC3.2.

[b]Parentheses denotes decrease.

Alternatively, days of developed skiing per participant are projected to decrease by an average of 32 percent, or by about 2 days per participant annually, by 2060. This decrease is somewhat offset by population growth and the increase in number of participants, resulting in increased total skiing days annually across all three climate scenarios (Table 19). For climate scenario CGCM3.1, in which average annual temperature rises the least and average annual precipitation increases the most, the increase in total skiing days is 39 percent. For the equally likely warmer dryer scenarios, CSIROMK3.5 and MIROC3.2, the increases in total annual days are less than 10 percent, despite the large expected increases in participants.

Undeveloped skiing—Undeveloped skiing often is pursued locally and does not require extensive recreation-site facilities. About 4.8 percent of northern adults, or 4.8 million people, engaged in undeveloped skiing in 2008. By 2060, this participation rate is projected to drop 27 to 41 percent, depending on the climate scenario (Table 20) with the warmer and drier MIROC3.2 showing the largest decrease. Other contributing factors include changing demographics in the region and declining public land per capita. Population growth would slightly offset the large decrease in participation rates, although on average the total number of participants in the region is projected to decrease by 11 percent, or about 0.6 million annually, by 2060.

Table 20—Projected undeveloped skiing (cross-country skiing, snowshoeing) by adults in the Northern United States, 2008 to 2060, under Resources Planning Act (RPA) scenario A1B and related climate futures.

RPA Scenario	2008	2060 Climate Average[a]	2060 Climate Average[a]	2060 CGCM3.1	2060 CSIRO-MK3.5	2060 MIROC3.2
	Per capita participation		Percent increase (decrease) from 2008			
A1B	0.048	0.032	(34)[b]	(35)	(27)	(41)
	Adult participants (millions)		Percent increase (decrease) from 2008			
A1B	4.8	4.2	(11)	(12)	(2)	(21)
	Days per participant		Percent increase (decrease) from 2008			
A1B	6.66	6.09	(9)	(9)	(9)	(8)
	Total days (millions)		Percent increase (decrease) from 2008			
A1B	32.1	26.0	(19)	(19)	(10)	(27)

[a]Result of average across CGCM3.1, CSIROMK3.5, and MIROC3.2.

[b]Parentheses denotes decrease.

Annual days per skier drop less than participation over the time period, less than 1 day per year, with little variation among climate scenarios. Thus, the predicted average 19-percent drop in undeveloped skiing days annually by 2060 appears to be primarily an artifact of the decreasing number of participants (Table 20). Overall, annual days of undeveloped skiing in the region are expected to decrease from 32.1 million to about 26 million by 2060.

Non-motorized water activities consist of swimming and various forms of non-motorized boating.

Swimming—Swimming includes various related activities such as snorkeling, surfing, diving, and visiting beaches or watersides. It is the fourth most popular outdoor activity in the North, with a 63.3-percent adult participation rate and about 62 million adult participants annually (Table 21).

Table 21—Projected swimming participation and use (family gathering, picnicking, developed camping) by adults in the Northern United States, 2008 to 2060, under Resources Planning Act (RPA) scenario A1B and related climate futures.

RPA Scenario	2008	2060 Climate Average[a]	2060 Climate Average[a]	2060 CGCM3.1	2060 CSIRO-MK3.5	2060 MIROC3.2
	Per capita participation		Percent increase (decrease) from 2008			
A1B	0.633	0.633	0	9	(4)[b]	(4)
	Adult participants (millions)		Percent increase (decrease) from 2008			
A1B	61.7	83.3	35	47	29	29
	Days per participant		Percent increase (decrease) from 2008			
A1B	22.24	21.13	(5)	2	(9)	(8)
	Total days (millions)		Percent increase (decrease) from 2008			
A1B	1,376.2	1,771.8	29	51	17	18

[a] *Result of average across CGCM3.1, CSIROMK3.5, and MIROC3.2.*

[b] *Parentheses denotes decrease.*

Table 22—Projected floating participation and use (canoeing, tubing, kayaking, rafting, sailing) by adults in the Northern United States, 2008 to 2060, under Resources Planning Act (RPA) scenario A1B and related climate futures.

RPA Scenario	2008	2060 Climate Average[a]	2060 Climate Average[a]	2060 CGCM3.1	2060 CSIRO-MK3.5	2060 MIROC3.2
	Per capita participation		Percent increase (decrease) from 2008			
A1B	0.187	0.157	(16)[b]	(3)	(24)	(21)
	Adult participants (millions)		Percent increase (decrease) from 2008			
A1B	18.2	20.7	14	31	3	6
	Days per participant		Percent increase (decrease) from 2008			
A1B	6.82	5.46	(20)	(8)	(25)	(27)
	Total days (millions)		Percent increase (decrease) from 2008			
A1B	124.0	114.2	(8)	21	(23)	(22)

[a] Result of average across CGCM3.1, CSIROMK3.5, and MIROC3.2.

[b] Parentheses denotes decrease.

On average, this participation rate is expected to remain constant over the projection period. Thus, the number of swimmers can be expected to increase by the same rate as the regional population. This would mean an increase of 17 to 29 million participants by 2060. Days per participant are projected to decrease slightly, 5 percent on average, under A1B and the three climate scenarios. Nevertheless, because of the high societal participation rate and the large number of days of annual engagement, swimming-related activities will likely increase 17 to 51 percent or by between 238 and 696 million days per year by 2060.

Floating—The adult participation rate for this non-motorized boating activity—including canoeing, kayaking, tubing, sailing, and whitewater (or other) rafting—averaged about 18.7 percent, or about 18.2 million participants, annually in the North from 2005 to 2009. Across the climate scenarios associated with A1B, the participation rate is expected to decrease 3 to 24 percent by 2060, with the warmer drier scenarios differing from CGCM3.1 by more than 20-percent (Table 22). On average, the 16 percent decrease in participation rate, coupled with population growth, would mean an increase in adult participants of about 14 percent, or 2.5 million people.

Annual days per participant, about 7 in 2008, are expected to decrease across all climate scenarios by 8 to 27 percent, with the drier and warmer climate forecasts roughly tripling the decrease in CGCM3.1. On average, the decrease would be about 20 percent or 1.4 days per participant annually in 2060. Total days of participation will likely increase by 21 percent under CGCM3.1, but decrease by 23 percent under CSIROMK3.5 and 22 percent under MIROC3.2. Thus, depending on the climate changes, annual total days of participation, which totaled 124 million in 2008, could be as low as 95 million or as high as 150 million, although on average a decrease of about 10 million participant days per year is expected.

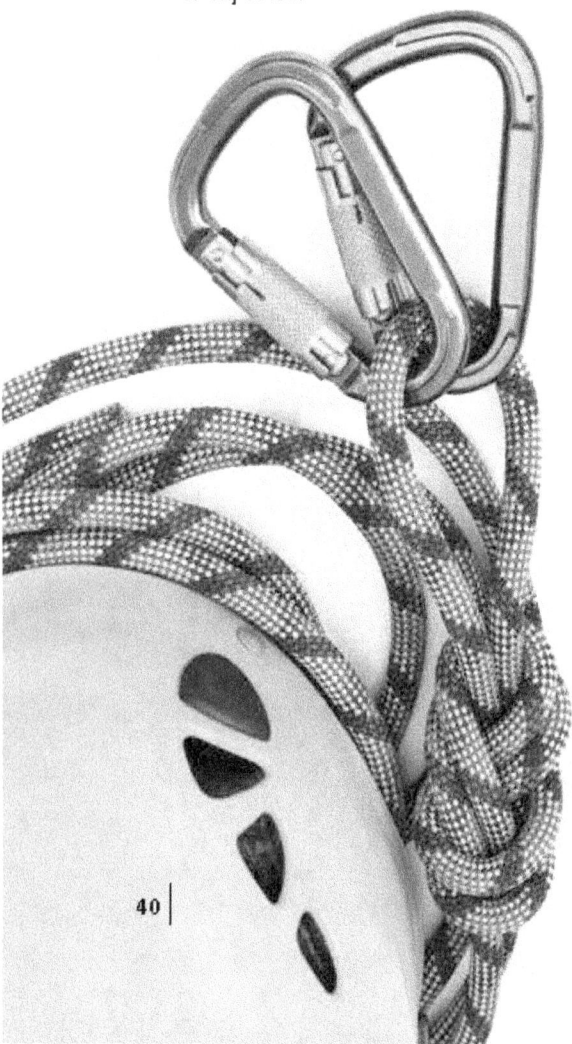

Outdoor recreation will remain important in the North over the next five decades. The number of participants in 14 of the 17 outdoor recreation activities, or activity aggregates, examined for this report is projected to increase (Table 23). For a number of activities, the per capita participation rate is expected to decrease, but, expected population growth under the A1B simulation (high economic growth and moderate population growth) would be large enough to ensure that only a few—hunting, snowmobiling, and undeveloped skiing—would actually experience a decrease in participants over the next five decades. Of these, snowmobiling and undeveloped skiing could experience large decreases relative to current participant numbers.

In general, participation intensity, or total days of participation, will likely mirror number of participants. Twelve of 17 activities are expected to experience an increase in annual participation days in 2060 compared to 2008 (Table 24). Under A1B, and averaging across the three climate scenarios, non-motorized boating, visiting primitive areas, hunting, snowmobiling, and undeveloped skiing are all likely to experience decreases in total days of participation. Of these, the two winter activities would see the biggest proportional drops, but hunting and visiting primitive areas would experience much larger absolute decreases. More specific discussions of participant numbers, days of participation, and the factors responsible follow.

Table 23—Changes in total outdoor recreation participation across 17 activities by adults in the Northern United States, 2008 to 2060, under Resources Planning Act (RPA) scenario A1B and related climate futures.

Activity	2008 Participants	2060 Participant Range[a]	2060 Participant Range[a]	2060 Average Participant Change[b]
	(millions)	(millions)	(percent)	(millions)
Developed site use				
Visiting developed sites (family gathering, picnicking, developed camping)	80.5	102 - 109	27 - 35	24
Visiting interpretive sites (nature centers, prehistoric sites, historic sites, other)	67.0	98 - 99	47 - 48	32
Observing nature				
Birding (viewing or photographing)	37.2	46 - 52	24 - 40	11
Nature viewing[c] (viewing or photographing birds, other wildlife, natural scenery, gathering, other)	79.5	105 - 111	32 - 39	28
Backcountry activities				
Challenge (mountain climbing, rock climbing, caving)	9.4	11 - 12	16 - 27	2
Equestrian (horseback riding on trails)	5.8	10 - 12	67 - 108	5
Day hiking	32.4	41 - 44	28 - 35	10
Primitive area use (visiting wilderness, primitive camping, backpacking)	36.1	32 - 44	(11)[d] - 22	1
Motorized activities				
Off-road driving	17.3	20 - 22	18 - 29	7
Motorized snow (snowmobiling)	7.0	2.1 - 4	(70) - (44)	(4)
Motorized water (motor boating, water skiing, personal watercraft use)	26.1	42 - 51	61 - 96	21
Hunting and fishing				
Hunting (all types of legal hunting)	11.3	8 - 11	(28) - 0	(2)
Fishing (warm water, cold water, saltwater, anadromous)	28.7	40 - 49	39 - 71	17

Table 23 continued

Activity	2008 Participants	2060 Participant Range[a]	2060 Participant Range[a]	2060 Average Participant Change[b]
	(millions)	(millions)	(percent)	(millions)
Non-motorized Winter				
Developed skiing (downhill skiing, snowboarding)	11.6	19 - 21	69 - 78	9
Undeveloped skiing (cross-country skiing, snowshoeing)	4.8	3.8 - 4.7	(21) - (2)	(0.6)
Non-motorized Water				
Swimming (screener for various swimming and related activities)	61.7	80 - 91	29 - 47	22
Floating (canoeing, kayaking, rafting, sailing)	18.2	19 - 24	3 - 31	3

[a]Participant range for RPA A1B and climate alternatives (CGCM3.1, CSIROMK3.5, MIROC3.2).

[b]Result of average across CGCM3.1, CSIROMK3.5, and MIROC3.2.

[c]Including birding.

[d]Parentheses denotes decrease or negative value.

Table 24—Changes in total outdoor recreation days across 17 activities by adults in the Northern United States, 2008 to 2060, under Resources Planning Act (RPA) scenario A1B and related climate futures.

Activity	2008 Days	2060 Days Range[a]	2060 Days Range[a]	2060 Average Days Change
	(millions)	(millions)	(percent)	(millions)
Developed site use				
Visiting developed sites (family gathering, picnicking, developed camping)	943	1,054 - 1,201	12 - 27	163
Visiting interpretive sites (nature centers, prehistoric sites, historic sites, other)	516	820 - 887	59 - 72	343
Observing nature				
Birding (viewing or photographing)	3,696	4,413 - 5,006	19 - 35	929
Nature viewing[c] (viewing or photographing birds, other wildlife, natural scenery, gathering, other)	13,925	16,548 - 17,730	19 - 27	3,104
Backcountry activities				
Challenge (mountain climbing, rock climbing, caving)	37.7	42 - 48	12 - 27	7
Equestrian (horseback riding on trails)	72.3	119 - 144	65 - 100	61
Day hiking	723.8	846 - 923	17 - 28	162
Primitive area use (visiting wilderness, primitive camping, backpacking)	415	282 - 435	(32)[d] - 5	(73)
Motorized activities				
Off-road driving	282.8	291 - 327	3 - 16	24
Motorized snow (snowmobiling)	54.8	15 - 26	(74) - (52)	(35)
Motorized water (motor boating, water skiing, personal watercraft use)	378.8	651 - 827	72 - 118	374
Hunting and fishing				
Hunting (all types of legal hunting)	209.6	121 - 184	(42) - (12)	(64)

Table 24 continued

Activity	2008 Days	2060 Days Range[a]	2060 Days Range[a]	2060 Average Days Change[b]
	(millions)	(millions)	(percent)	(millions)
Fishing (warm water, cold water, saltwater, anadromous)	515.7	719 - 1,052	39 - 104	404
Non-motorized Winter				
Developed skiing (downhill skiing, snowboarding)	81.3	86 - 113	6 - 39	15
Undeveloped skiing (cross-country skiing, snowshoeing)	32.1	23 - 29	(27) - (10)	(6)
Non-motorized Water				
Swimming (screener for various swimming and related activities)	1,376.2	1,614 - 2,072	17 - 51	396
Floating (canoeing, kayaking, rafting, sailing)	124	96 - 150	(23) - 21	(10)

[a] *Days range for RPA A1B and climate alternatives (CGCM3.1, CSIROMK3.5, MIROC3.2).*

[b] *Result of average across CGCM3.1, CSIROMK3.5, and MIROC3.2.*

[c] *Including birding.*

[d] *Parentheses denotes decrease or negative value.*

Per capita participation— In the next 50 years, under A1B and related climate scenarios for the North, the outdoor recreation activities projected for the most growth in per capita participation (Fig. 7) are developed skiing (25 to 32 percent), horseback riding (23 to 54 percent), fishing (3 to 27 percent), motorized water use (20 to 45 percent), and visiting interpretive areas (9 percent).

A number of activities are projected to experience decreases in adult participation rates. The five activities with the biggest participation rate decreases (Fig. 8) are floating (3 to 24 percent), hunting (26 to 47 percent), snowmobiling (58 to 78 percent), primitive-area visiting (10 to 34 percent), and undeveloped skiing (27 to 41 percent).

FIGURE 7

Recreation activities with the highest projected growth in participation rate, 2008 to 2060, in the Northern United States under a future of high economic growth and moderate population growth (A1B) and an average of climate scenarios predicted by three general circulation models: CGCM3.1, CSIROMK3.5, and MIROC3.2. (source: 2010 Resources Planning Act assessment).

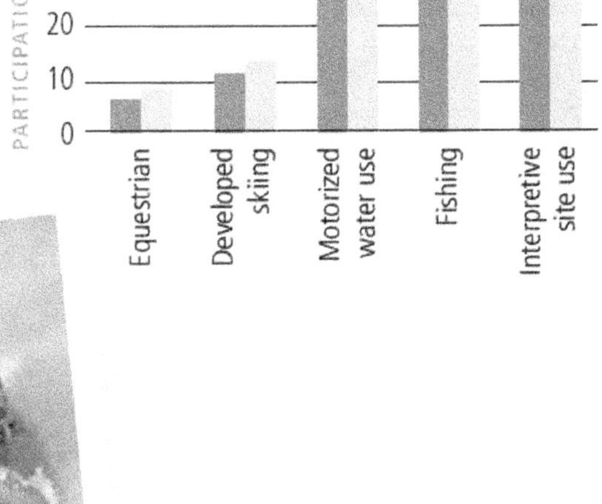

FIGURE 8

Recreation activities with the lowest projected growth in participation rate, 2008 to 2060, in the Northern United States under a future of high economic growth and moderate population growth (A1B) and an average of climate scenarios predicted by three general circulation models: CGCM3.1, CSIROMK3.5, and MIROC3.2. (source: 2010 Resources Planning Act assessment).

Figure 7: PARTICIPATION RATE (percent of adults). Categories: Equestrian, Developed skiing, Motorized water use, Fishing, Interpretive site use. Legend: 2008, 2060.

Figure 8: PARTICIPATION RATE (percent of adults). Categories: Undeveloped skiing, Motorized snow use (snowmobiling), Hunting, Floating (canoeing, kayaking, rafting, sailing), Primitive area use. Legend: 2008, 2060.

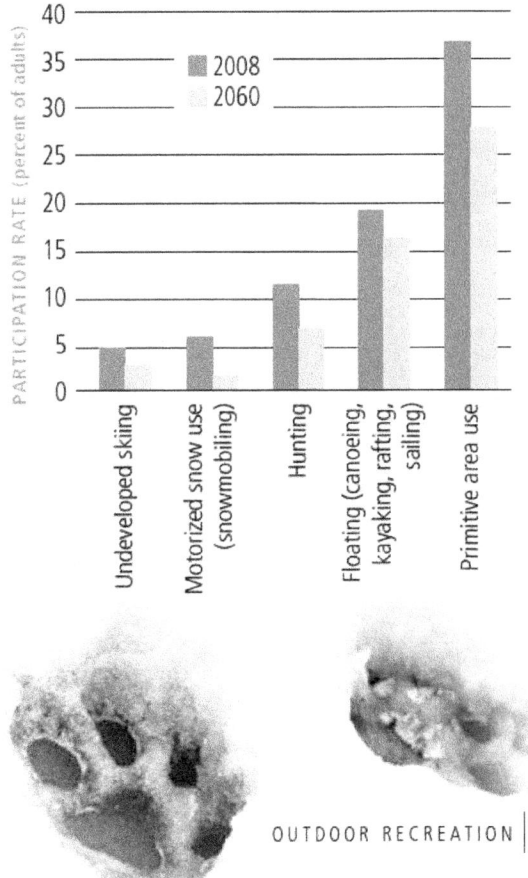

Change in participation rates for the remaining activities studied in this report will likely be marginal, vacillating around zero. Generally, activities with currently low per capita rates of participation, such as downhill skiing and horseback riding, have considerable room for growth (decline), but activities with already high participation rates, such as developed site use, nature viewing, and swimming, have less room for growth (decline). Thus, the larger percentage changes in predicted participation rates are often for the currently less popular activities.

Participant numbers—Participant numbers follow the predicted trends of participation rates as they are simply the product of participation rate and population. Across climate scenarios (Table 23), the highest growth rates for participant numbers are expected for developed skiing (69 to 78 percent), horseback riding (67 to 108 percent), fishing (39 to 71 percent), motorized water use (61 to 96 percent), and visiting interpretive areas (47 to 48 percent).

A number of activities will likely show less growth and experience decreases in adult participation rates. The five activities that are expected to experience the least growth in participant numbers are non-motorized boating (3 to 31 percent increase), hunting (0 percent growth to 28 percent decrease), snowmobiling (44 to 70 percent decrease), primitive-area visiting (22 percent growth to 11 percent decrease), and undeveloped skiing (2 to 21 percent decrease).

Although growth rates for participant numbers are important, a potentially more important measure for natural resource managers is change in absolute numbers of participants. Activities with already high participation rates often do not demonstrate large percentage changes in participant numbers. However, smaller percentage changes in already highly popular activities can mean quite large changes in the absolute number of adult participants.

The activities that are expected to show the biggest average increases from 2008 to 2060 in participants (Table 23) are visiting developed sites (24 million), nature viewing (28 million), interpretive-area visiting (32 million), swimming (22 million), motorized water use (21 million) and fishing (17 million). These are among the most popular activities examined in this report. Activities expected to have the smallest participant increases across climate scenarios on average, some with participant number decreases, include challenge activities (2 million increase), floating (3 million increase), hunting (2 million decrease), primitive area use (1 million increase), snowmobiling (4 million decrease), and undeveloped skiing (slightly more than 0.5 million decrease).

Participant days per year—As described in eq. 3, average activity days per year per participant are used in conjunction with participation rate and population to determine total activity days per year. Yearly days per participant are projected to decrease for most outdoor recreation activities from 2008 to 2060. Three activities, visiting interpretive sites, motorized boating, and fishing are expected to experience increases across the climate scenarios, with average annual days per participant climbing to between 8 and 9 days for visiting interpretive sites and climbing to around 16 days for motorized boating, and to 20 days on average for fishing. Challenge activities will likely maintain about the same number of annual days per participant in 2060 as in 2008.

All other activities are expected to experience a decrease in days per participant per year, with the largest decreases in developed skiing (32 percent), visiting primitive areas (21 percent), and floating (20 percent). For nature viewing, with a 2008 average of about 176 days per year, a 9 percent decrease by 2060 could translate into an average of 16 fewer activity days per year. However, for activities where participants engage less often, the decreases would be less, less than 1 day per year for snowmobiling and approximately 2 days per year for hunting. For the remaining activities, the changes, although negative, are expected to be relatively minor.

Total activity days per year—Total days are the product of population, participation rate, and days per participant. The five fastest growing outdoor activities, in total days from 2008 to 2060 (Table 24 and Fig. 9), are predicted to be horseback riding (65 to 100 percent), fishing (39 to 104 percent), interpretive-area visiting (59 to 72 percent), motorized water use (72 to 118 percent), and swimming (17 to 51 percent). Alternatively, the five slowest growing activities (Fig. 10) are predicted to be off-road driving (3 to 16 percent increase), primitive area use (5 percent increase to 32 percent decrease), undeveloped skiing (10 to 27 percent decrease), hunting (12 to 42 percent decrease), and snowmobiling (52 to 74 percent decrease).

Higher growth rates do not necessarily imply larger absolute growth. Activities that are currently popular may have slower rates of growth in total days than less popular alternatives, yet their increase in total days may greatly exceed those for less popular but faster growing activities. Averaged over all climate scenarios for A1B, the five activities for which total days would increase the most over the next 50 years (Table 24) are nature viewing (3,104 million days), birding (929 million days), fishing (404 million days), swimming (396 million days) motorized water use (374 million days), and visiting interpretive sites (343 million). Day hiking (162 million days) and visiting developed sites (163 million days) are the only other activities for which days per year are expected to increase by more than 100 million per year by 2060.

FIGURE 9

Recreation activities with the highest projected growth in total consumption, 2008 to 2060, in the Northern United States under a future of high economic growth and moderate population growth (A1B) and an average of climate scenarios predicted by three general circulation models: CGCM3.1, CSIROMK3.5, and MIROC3.2. (source: 2010 Resources Planning Act assessment).

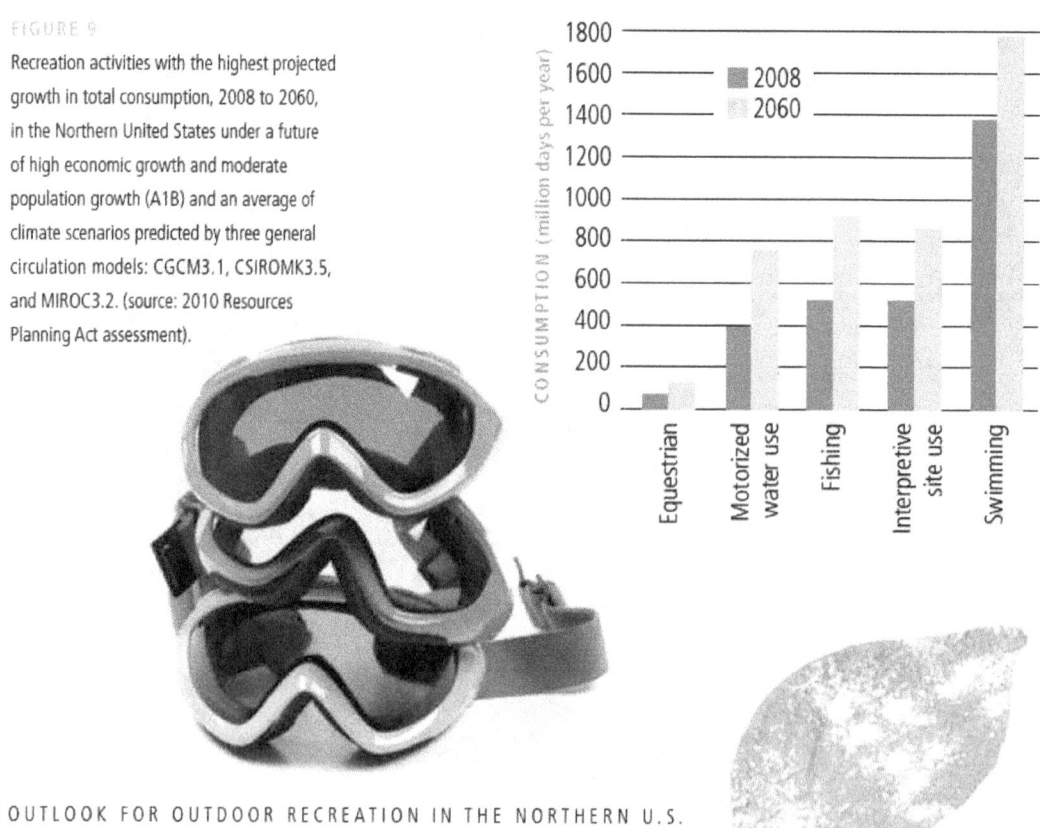

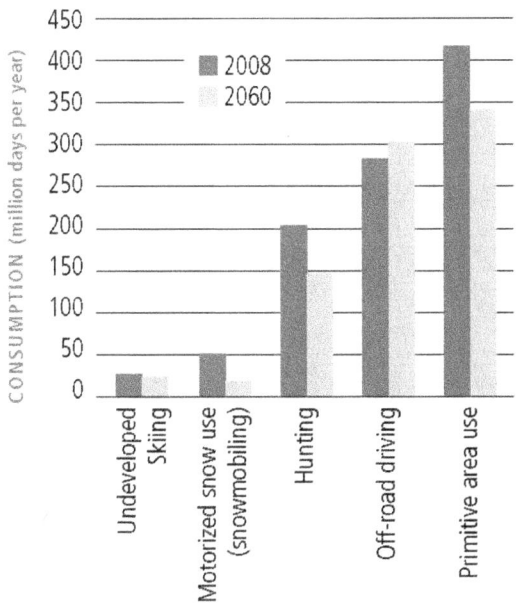

FIGURE 10

Recreation activities with the lowest projected growth in total consumption, 2008 to 2060, in the Northern United States under a future of high economic growth and moderate population growth (A1B) and an average of climate scenarios predicted by three general circulation models: CGCM3.1, CSIROMK3.5, and MIROC3.2. (source: 2010 Resources Planning Act assessment).

Alternatively, five activities are projected to decrease in total activity days per year by 2060 when averaged across all climate scenarios for A1B (Table 24): floating (10 million days), hunting (64 million days), primitive area use (73 million days), snowmobiling (35 million days), and undeveloped skiing (6 million days). These activities are typically space intensive and generally require investments in equipment and training. Moreover, the two winter activities require some level of snow cover.

Climate scenarios—Participant numbers and days of participation were projected for A1B with associated climate scenarios (Fig. 6). Details about climate effects on recreation participation and use can be observed in Tables 6 to 22. No specific probabilities were assigned to any of the three climate scenarios associated with A1B (Joyce et al., in press).

However, the general effects of climate change on each of the 17 outdoor recreation activities examined in this report can be inferred by comparing the percent increases or decreases in Tables 6 to 22. For most activities, the scenarios that are warmer and drier on average over the next five decades (CISROMK3.5 and MIROC3.2) predict lower participation rates, with the largest effects predicted for hunting, snowmobiling, and undeveloped skiing. Alternatively, activities such as horseback riding, motorized water use, and fishing would likely experience relatively higher participation rates under the warmer and drier climate scenarios. For other activities—like visiting interpretive sites, nature viewing, and developed skiing—differences across climate scenarios would be marginal. The general effects of climate change on projections of total days can be similarly observed in the percent increases or decreases in Tables 6 to 22. The pattern is generally the same as with participation.

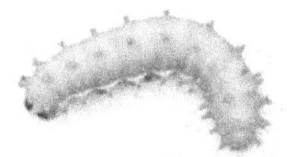

Examination of model results and odds ratio estimates in the Appendix reveals findings similar to previous research into outdoor recreation participation behavior. First, men are more apt than women to participate in backcountry activities, hunting, fishing, motorized activities, snowmobiling, and floating; and women are more likely to participate in nature viewing, swimming, horseback riding, and visiting interpretive sites.

Ethnicity appears highly associated with participation but it is less a factor on the annual days of participation once an individual has chosen to participate. Minorities, including African Americans, Hispanic Americans, and Asian Americans, are almost always less likely than Caucasians to participate in the activities examined in this report. Respondents claiming Native American, Non-Hispanic identity are often more likely than Caucasians to participate in the remote activities, such as hunting, fishing, off-road driving, snowmobiling, hiking, horseback riding, and nature viewing. These

results are similar to previous studies relating ethnicity to recreation participation. A notable exception is day hiking; controlling for other socioeconomic and supply factors, participation is more likely for Hispanic Americans than Caucasians.

Education beyond high school generally resulted in higher participation rates for most activities, but not for all. For example, the higher the education level, the higher the likelihood of participation in birding, non-motorized winter activities, backcountry activities, and nature viewing. However, for fishing and hunting, off-road driving, and snowmobiling, having an education beyond high school is associated with a lowered probability of participation.

Income is positively associated with participation and use across all activities. For some activities—such as birding, hiking, and hunting—the effect was small, but was large for developed skiing and motorized water use. An important aspect of income growth that was not addressed in our analysis for this report should also be mentioned. The RPA assessment variables used in this study were limited to aggregate income growth without regard to changing income distribution over the simulation period. This omission is potentially serious and may overlook the possibility of outdoor recreation access becoming more partitioned by income class.

Relevant land and water availability per capita generally relate positively to activity participation. Hence, decreases in overall forest and rangeland per capita, Federal land per capita, and National Wilderness Preservation System lands per capita produce decreases in spatially intensive activities, such as horseback riding, hunting, motorized off-road driving, visiting primitive areas, and nature viewing.

Similarly, participation in water-based activities, such as swimming, motorized water use, and non-motorized water use, is positively related to the per capita availability of water area. Fishing participation is positively influenced by both water area and forest and rangeland availability. A seemingly counterintuitive result occurs with the variable indicating whether the respondent lives in a coastal community: participation in fishing, hunting, and nature viewing are negatively related to residence in a coastal county, a result that might be driven by the urban dominance of the northern coastal population.

LIMITATIONS IN MODEL RESULTS

The model results and projections in this chapter do not account for factors outside the range of available data such as new technology, changes in relative costs, changing site congestion conditions, new infrastructure, acculturation, generational trends, and changes in tastes and preferences. Hence, for an activity like developed skiing, projections of relatively large participant increases could be dampened significantly by declining quality or potentially increased access price that would result from overcrowding combined with declining carrying capacity on areas experiencing climate-induced spatial and temporal limitations. Moreover, the effects of climate on fish and game species were not developed fully enough to include as feedbacks into our behavioral models.

Some other caveats:

- Despite having up to a decade of data for model development, our dataset was not large enough for establishment of any meaningful or statistically significant time-varying parametric relationships. Thus, the participation and days models were static, a substantial limitation when projecting demand over such long time intervals.

- Simulated projections were limited by the quality of the projected exogenous variables.

- The sample of respondents was limited to adults (16 years and older); thus, the effects of recreation demand by youth were omitted. For activities that are traditionally adult in nature—such as challenge sports, visiting primitive areas, and hunting—omitting children is likely not a serious omission. However, for visiting developed sites, swimming, fishing, visiting interpretive areas, and other family-oriented activities, the results presented herein could be biased somewhat downward relative to overall use.

- By performing the analyses at the regional level, we may have overlooked important subregional changes and resulting implications. For example, visiting a primitive or wilderness area or day hiking may have a different meaning for a rural resident than an urbanite.

Conclusions

Under the demographic, land use, and climate conditions that we considered for this report, recreation participant numbers and days in the field will likely grow for most activities over the next 50 years. Thus, the general outlook for outdoor recreation resources in the North is a per capita reduction in opportunities and access.

Assuming that the public land base for outdoor recreation remains stable and the privately owned land base available for recreation decreases, an increasing population would result in decreasing opportunities for recreation per person across most of the region. Although many other factors are involved in recreation supply, recreation resources (both natural and constructed) likely will become less "available" as more people compete to use them.

On privately owned land, increased competition for recreational resources resulting from increased demand relative to supply could mean rising access prices. On public lands, where access fees cannot be adjusted easily to market or quasi-market conditions, increased congestion and possible decreases in the quality of the outdoor recreation experience are likely to present important challenges to management.

A major challenge for natural resource managers and planners will be to ensure that recreation opportunities remain viable and that they grow along with the population. This challenge will probably have to be met through creative and efficient management of site attribute inputs and plans, rather than through any major expansions or additions to the natural resource base. Trends toward more flexible work scheduling and telecommuting may allow recreationists to allocate their leisure time more evenly across the seasons and through the week, thus facilitating less concentrated peak demands. As well, entrepreneurs and managers may identify opportunities for more efficiently using resources by expanding seasonal opportunities, for example developing mountain biking venues at ski areas.[1] Conversely, such technological innovations as global positioning system units and inexpensive plastic kayaks would allow people to find and get to places more easily and quickly, perhaps leading to overuse pressures not previously considered a threat.

---

[1] *D.J. Mansius, director, Forest Policy & Management, Maine Forest Service, Dept. of Conservation. Personal communication. August 17, 2012.*

Overall, a future in which the infrastructure supporting the region's outdoor recreation opportunities will not be severely tested is hard to envision. For activities like improved-facility use and day hiking, fewer acres or trail miles per participant could begin to strain existing infrastructure as biological and social carrying capacities are exceeded. Some activities may not require expansive contiguous areas for quality experiences; examples are birding, which is often "edge dependent," and hiking, which occurs along linear corridors. However, activities typically considered space intensive—horseback riding on trails, motorized water use, fishing, and off-road driving—are likely to actually "feel" much more congested given the nature of the activity. Alternatively, activities like hunting and primitive area use could feel considerably less congested because of projected decreases in annual user days.

Measures of use per acre or other units of infrastructure are not comparable across recreation activities, and some may actually have a social component—with more congestion yielding increased user utility—but only up to a point. For activities that may be near carrying capacity from a recreation user perspective, or infrastructure carrying capacity, large increases in use per acre could be a concern, both for the land and for the user. Increased pressure can be expected on fishery resources, water quantity, and water quality in areas used for motor boating and at interpretive areas.

Because general forest area recreation usage—including hunting, off-road driving, fishing, and horseback riding on trails—generally require more space per user for high quality (and safe) experiences, an increase in use density would undoubtedly be of concern to national forest managers. For example, conflicts arising from congestion may increase, not only within an activity (such as off-road drivers running into each other figuratively and literally) but also across activities (such as off-road drivers spooking horses and scaring away game sought by hunters). Managers of general forest areas may have to choose among potentially unpopular access regulation schemes to mitigate conflicts. They may also need to consider sectioning general forest areas into special use areas for specific activities—such as off-road driving, horseback riding on trails, and hunting—to reduce cross-activity congestion conflicts. Needless to say, the increased congestion can only increase the impacts of recreation on the forest environment.

Choices in outdoor recreation activities have changed over time in response to changing tastes and preferences, demographics, technological innovations, economic conditions, and changing recreational opportunities. Overall, the number of nature-based outdoor recreation participants has increased since the last RPA assessment, continuing a long-term trend. At the same time, recreation visitation to State parks and Federal lands has apparently not increased at similar rates, indicating that recreationists are also using other resources.

The change in recreation preferences at least partly reflects changing demographics in the U.S. public. As the northern population ages and becomes more racially and ethnically diverse, no one can predict with certainty how future recreation demand and supply will adjust. Based on the available data, we nevertheless project future growth for most recreation activities. Future demand, of course, can be expected to change as relative costs, competition for access, and other scarcity factors change and affect choices for recreation activities, times, and locations.

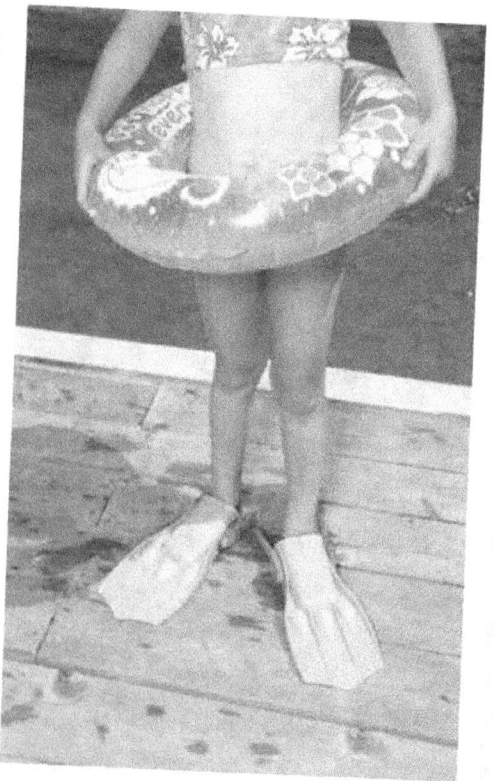

Climate can affect willingness to participate in recreation activities as well as recreation resource availability and quality. The climate variables that we used in the recreation models were limited to those from the RPA assessment or were derivatives of those basic variables. Generally, these variables were presumed to affect willingness to participate and frequency of participation directly. However, even without existing data, climate change might be expected to affect resource availability, directly and indirectly. For example, increasing temperatures will likely affect the distribution of plant and animal species fundamental to maintaining fish and game populations. Moreover, changes in precipitation may influence local snow cover and thus affect seasonal availability for such activities as snowmobiling and undeveloped skiing. Walls et al. (2009) concluded that the single most important new challenge to recreation supply will be mitigating the adverse effects of climate change, particularly in coastal areas and on western public lands. Because disentangling the effects of the climate variables on recreation participation is difficult, further exploration of these direct and indirect relationships—at both local and macro levels—will be fundamental to improving future forecasts.

Acknowledgments

The authors are grateful to Karen Abt, Ross Arnold, Melissa Baker, Don English, Linda Langner, Ed O'Leary, Donald Mansius, Evan Mercer, Neelam Poudyal, Steve Shifley, John Stanovick, Eric White, Carol Whitlock, and Stan Zarnoch for helpful suggestions toward the development of this report. Also thanks to Linda Joyce for providing climate data; to David Wear for providing land use data; to Ken Cordell and Carter Betz for providing recreation participation and supply data, 2005 to 2009 averages for participant and days numbers by activity, and insights on recreation trends; and to Shela Mou for her valuable assistance in manuscript preparation.

We thank them all

Literature Cited

Alcamo, J.; Ash, N.J.; Butler, C.D.; [et al.]. 2003. Ecosystems and human well-being. Washington, DC: Island Press. 245 p.

Bowker, J.M. 2001. Outdoor recreation participation and use by Alaskans: projections 2000-2020. Gen. Tech. Rep. PNW–GTR–527. Portland, OR: U.S. Department of Agriculture, Forest Service, Pacific Northwest Research Station. 28 p.

Bowker, J.M.; Askew, A.E.; Cordell, H.K.; Bergstrom, J.C. In press. Outdoor Recreation. In: Wear, D.N. and J.G. Greis, eds. Southern Forest Futures Project. Gen. Tech. Rep. Asheville, NC: U.S. Department of Agriculture, Forest Service, Southern Research Station.

Bowker, J.M.; Askew, A.E.; Cordell, H.K.; [et al.]. 2012. Outdoor Recreation Participation in the United States – Projections to 2060: A technical document supporting the Forest Service 2010 Resources Planning Act Assessment. Gen. Tech. Rep. SRS-160. Asheville, NC: U.S. Department of Agriculture, Forest Service, Southern Research Station. 36 p.

Bowker, J.M.; Bergstrom, J.C.; Gill, J. 2007. Estimating the economic value and impacts of recreational trails: a case study of the Virginia Creeper rail trail. Tourism Economics. 13: 241–260.

Bowker, J.M.; Bergstrom, J.C.; Starbuck, C.M. [et al.]. 2010. Estimating demographic and population level induced changes in recreation demand for outdoor recreation on US national forests: an application of National Visitor Use Monitoring Program data. Fac. Ser. Work. Pap. FS 1001. Athens, GA: University of Georgia, Department of Agricultural and Applied Economics. 147 p.

Bowker, J.M.; English, D.B.K.; Cordell, H.K. 1999. Outdoor recreation participation and consumption: projections 2000 to 2050. In: Cordell, H.K.; Betz, C.J.; Bowker, J.M.; [et al.]. Outdoor recreation in American life: a national assessment of demand and supply trends. Champagne, IL: Sagamore Press: 323–350.

Bowker, J.M.; Leeworthy, V.R. 1998. Accounting for ethnicity in recreation demand: a flexible count data approach. Journal of Leisure Research. 30: 64–78.

Bowker, J.M.; Murphy, D.; Cordell, H.K.; [et al.]. 2006. Wilderness and primitive area recreation participation and consumption: an examination of demographic and spatial factors. Journal of Agricultural and Applied Economics. 38(2): 317–326.

Cameron, C.A.; Trivedi, P.K. 1998. Econometric society monographs: regression analysis of count data. New York: Cambridge University Press. 412 p.

Cicchetti, C.J. 1973. Forecasting recreation in the United States. Lexington, MA: D.C. Heath and Co. 200 p.

Cordell, H.K., ed. 2012. Outdoor recreation trends and futures: a technical document supporting the Forest Service 2010 RPA assessment. Gen. Tech. Rep. SRS–150. Asheville, NC: U.S. Department of Agriculture, Forest Service, Southern Research Station. 167 p.

Cordell, H.K.; Bergstrom, J.C. 1991. A methodology for assessing national outdoor recreation demand and supply trends. Leisure Sciences. 13(1): 1–20.

Cordell, H.K.; Bergstrom, J.C.; Hartmann, L.A.; English, D.B.K. 1990. An analysis of the outdoor recreation and wilderness situation in the United States: 1989-2040. Gen. Tech. Rep. RM–189. Fort Collins, CO: U.S. Department of Agriculture, Forest Service, Rocky Mountain Forest and Range Experiment Station. 112 p.

Cordell, H.K.; Betz, C.J.; Zarnoch, S.J. 2013. Recreation and protected land resources in the United States: a technical document supporting the Forest Service 2010 RPA Assessment. Gen. Tech. Rep. SRS–169. Asheville, NC: U.S. Department of Agriculture, Forest Service, Southern Research Station. 198 p.

Cordell, H.K.; Betz, C.J.; Mou, S.H.; Gormanson, D. 2012. Outdoor recreation in a shifting northern societal landscape. Gen. Tech. Rep. NRS-100. Newtown Square, PA: U.S. Department of Agriculture, Forest Service, Northern Research Station. 74 p.

Dale, D.; Weaver, T. 1974. Trampling effects on vegetation of the trail corridors of north Rocky Mountain forests. Journal of Applied Ecology. 11: 767-772.

Englin, J.E.; Shonkwiler, J.S. 1995. Estimating social welfare using count data models: an application to long-run recreation demand under conditions of endogenous stratification and truncation. Review of Economics and Statistics. 77(1): 104–112.

English, D.B.K.; Betz, C.J.; Young, M.J. 1993. Regional demand and supply projections for outdoor recreation. Gen. Tech. Rep. RM–230. Fort Collins, CO: U.S. Department of Agriculture, Forest Service, Rocky Mountain Forest and Range Experiment Station. 44 p.

English, D.B.K.; Kocis, S.M.; Zarnoch, S.J.; Arnold, J.R. 2002. Forest Service national visitor use monitoring process: research method documentation. Gen. Tech. Rep. SRS–57. Asheville, NC: U.S. Department of Agriculture, Forest Service, Southern Research Station. 14 p.

Greene, W.H. 2009. NLOGIT 4.0. Plainview, NY: Econometric Software, Inc.

Hagerty, D.; Moeltner, K. 2005. Specification of driving costs in models of recreation demand. Land Economics. 81(1):127-143.

Hall, C.M.; Page, S.J. 1999. The geography of tourism and recreation. New York, NY: Routledge. 309 p.

Hall, T.E.; Heaton, H.; Kruger, L.E. 2009. Outdoor recreation in the Pacific Northwest and Alaska: trends in activity participation. Gen. Tech. Rep. PNW–778. Portland, OR: U.S. Department of Agriculture, Forest Service, Pacific Northwest Research Station. 108 p.

Hof, J.G.; Kaiser, H.F. 1983a. Long term outdoor recreation participation projections for public land management agencies. Journal of Leisure Research. 15(1): 1–14.

Hof, J.G; Kaiser, H.F. 1983b. Projections of future forest recreation use. Resour. Bull. WO–2. Washington, DC: U.S. Department of Agriculture, Forest Service. 12 p.

Intergovernmental Panel on Climate Change (IPCC). 2007. Climate change 2007, the fourth IPCC assessment report. http://www.ipcc.ch/publications_and_data/publications_and_data_reports.shtml (10 January 2013).

Joyce, L.A.; Price; D.T.; Coulson, D.P.; [et al.]. [In press]. Projecting climate change in the United States: a technical document supporting the Forest Service 2010 RPA Assessment. Gen. Tech. Rep. RMRS. Fort Collins, CO: U.S. Department of Agriculture, Forest Service, Rocky Mountain Research Station.

Leeworthy, V.R.; Bowker, J.M.; Hospital, J.D.; Stone, E.A. 2005. Projected participation in marine recreation: 2005 & 2010. Report prepared for U.S. Department of Commerce, National Oceanic and Atmospheric Administration, National Ocean Service, Special Projects Division, Silver Spring, MD. 152 p. Available at http://www.srs.fs.usda.gov/pubs/ja/ja_leeworthy002.pdf (10 January 2013).

Manning, R. E. 1997. Social carrying capacity of parks and outdoor recreation areas. Parks and Recreation. 32(10): 32-38.

Nakićenović, N.; Alcamo, J.; Davis, G.; [et al.]. 2000. Emissions scenarios. a special report of working group III of the Intergovernmental Panel on Climate Change. Cambridge, United Kingdom and New York, NY, USA: Cambridge University Press. 599 p. Available at http://www.grida.no/climate/ipcc/emission/index.htm (10 January 2013).

Ovaskainen, V.; Mikkola, J.; Pouta, E. 2001. Estimating recreation demand with on-site data: an application of truncated and endogenously stratified count data models. Journal of Forest Economics. 7(2): 125–144.

Poudyal, N.C.; Cho, S.H.; Bowker, J.M. 2008. Demand for resident hunting in the southeastern United States. Human Dimensions of Wildlife 13: 154-178.

SAS Institute Inc. 2004. SAS/STAT 9.1 user's guide. Cary, NC: SAS Institute Inc. 5,121 p.

Souter, R.A.; Bowker, J.M. 1996. A note on nonlinearity bias and dichotomous choice CVM: implications for aggregate benefits estimation. Agricultural and Resource Economics Review. 25(1): 54–59.

U.S. Census Bureau. 2004. U.S. interim projections by age, sex, race and Hispanic origin. http://www.census.gov/population/projections/. Washington, DC: U.S. Department of Commerce, Census Bureau. (10 January 2013).

U.S. Department of Agriculture Forest Service. 2009. National survey on recreation and the environment [Dataset]. Asheville, NC: U.S. Department of Agriculture, Forest Service. Available at www.srs.fs.usda.gov/trends/nsre/nsre2.html. (15 September 2010).

U.S. Department of Agriculture Forest Service. 2010. National Visitor Use Monitoring Program: FY 2009 NVUM national summary report. Washington, DC: U.S. Department of Agriculture, Forest Service. Available at www.fs.fed.us/recreation/programs/nvum/. (6 October 2010).

U.S. Department of Agriculture Forest Service. 2012. Future Scenarios: A technical document supporting the Forest Service 2010 RPA Assessment. Gen. Tech. Rept. RMRS–272. Fort Collins, CO: U.S. Department of Agriculture, Forest Service, Rocky Mountain Research Station. 34 p.

U.S. Department of Commerce Bureau of Economic Analysis. 2008a. National and income product accounts table 1.15. Gross domestic product. Version January 30, 2008. Washington, DC: U.S. Department of Commerce, Bureau of Economic Analysis.

U.S. Department of Commerce Bureau of Economic Analysis. 2008b. National and income product accounts table 2.1. Personal income and its disposition. Version January 30, 2008. Washington, DC: U.S. Department of Commerce, Bureau of Economic Analysis.

Walls, M.; Darley, S.; Siikamaki, J. 2009. The state of the great outdoors: America's parks, public lands, and recreation resources. Washington, DC: Resources for the Future. 97 p.

Walsh, R.G.; Jon, K.H.; McKean, J.R.; Hof, J. 1992. Effect of price on forecasts of participation in fish and wildlife recreation: an aggregate demand model. Journal of Leisure Research. 21: 140–156.

Wear, David N. 2011. Forecasts of county-level land uses under three future scenarios: a technical document supporting the Forest Service 2010 RPA Assessment. Gen. Tech. Rep. SRS–141. Asheville, NC: U.S. Department of Agriculture, Forest Service, Southern Research Station. 41 p.

Zarnoch, S.J.; Cordell, H.K.; Betz, C.J.; Langner, L. 2010. Projecting county-level populations under three future scenarios: a technical document supporting the Forest Service 2010 RPA assessment. e-Gen. Tech. Rep. SRS–128. Asheville, NC: U.S. Department of Agriculture, Forest Service, Southern Research Station. 8 p.

Zawacki, W.T.; Marsinko, A.; Bowker, J.M. 2000. A travel cost analysis of economic use value of nonconsumptive wildlife recreation in the United States. Forest Science. 46(4): 496–505.

*Roasting the
perfect marshmallow*

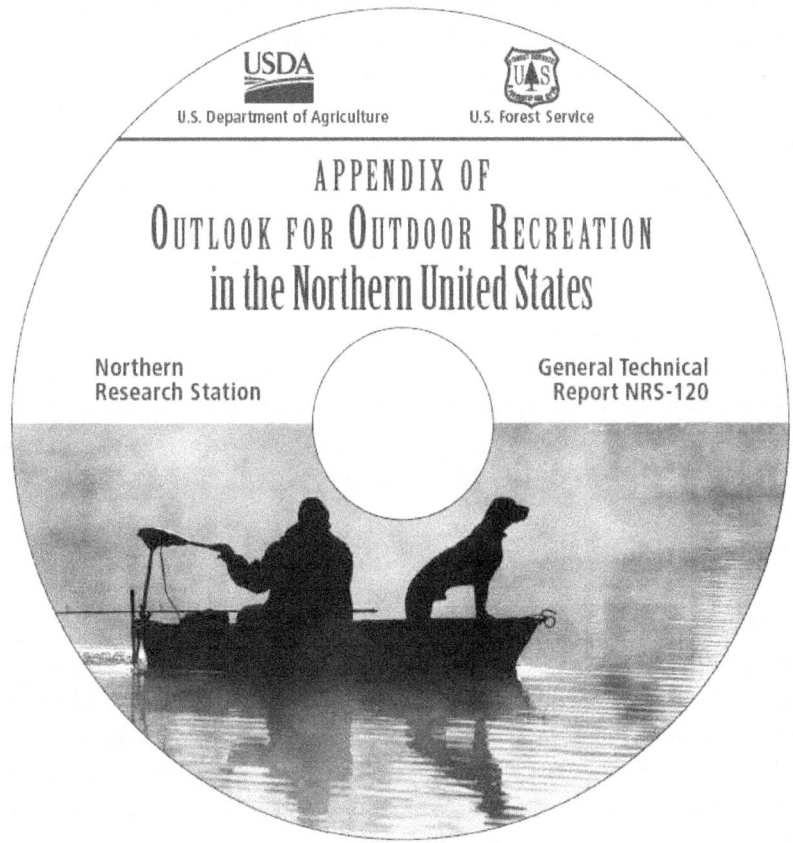

USDA
U.S. Department of Agriculture

U.S. Forest Service

APPENDIX OF
OUTLOOK FOR OUTDOOR RECREATION
in the Northern United States

Northern
Research Station

General Technical
Report NRS-120

We acknowledge the following photographers:

Page 15, top photo: Jasonn Beckstrand, U.S. Forest Service.

Page 28, bottom photo: Dave Schmid, U.S. Forest Service.

Page 50, bottom photo: Katie Carroll/Lindsay Campbell, U.S. Forest Service.

Page 52, bottom left photo: Barbara McGuinness, U.S. Forest Service.

U.S. Department of Agriculture

U.S. Forest Service

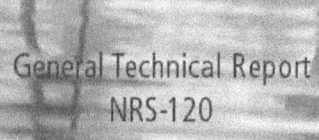

General Technical Report
NRS-120
2013